CONTEN

ACKNOWLEDGEMENTS

The kids of Canongate Youth Project; Panmure House; Fisherrow Centre; Longniddry Youth Club; Whitburn I.T. Group and others throughout the Lothians and Strathclyde deserve our thanks. They didn't exactly realise that they were being experimented on. Many enjoyed the games and tricks, and where they responded by showing us games and tricks, the circle was completed.

Alison Nimmo suffered, survived and did a grand job throughout the typing and preparation of the manuscript. **You** haven't seen our handwriting! Roly Wilson and Tony Day provided some of the diagrams and best of all, Jerry Neville visually uplifted our work by providing us with his humourous line-illustrations. Frank Booton is thanked for reading the manuscript and making corrections and suggestions. The same thanks go to our Scottish colleagues, Keith Simpson, Ian Taylor, Tom Scott and Gwynned Lloyd who have all looked at the material and made useful suggestions. Mike Tait and Hamish Murphy at CYP, Louis Isbrand from East Lothian Community Education team and Mark Green at Dundee University all aided the compilation and testing of the material for the book.

Finally, our thanks to the Social Work Services Group and the Jubilee Trust for financially backing the whole undertaking.

Alan and Howie

1 introduction

INTRODUCTION

Since the late 1960's the notion of "games" has been used in an almost mystical way to describe a better, alternative way of working with young people. This, of course, is yet another example of navel contemplation. We have been talking about the esoteric little world of 'professional' youth and community and youth social work. In that world, the new discipline of group dynamics, with all its examples of role play and leadership style experiments etc. gave rise to a mythologising which has, through time, like in so many other instances, become a compartmentalised body of knowledge. The case in point could be seen as the birth of "Relationship Games" and their subsequent professionalisation. A number of courses were run in the early '70's which were either about the use of games (meaning the relationship-type) with young people or where games were used as exercises to aid group cohesion. The reality of the situation was that gradually almost all courses and conferences began to resemble one another in format.

"Split into small groups, lets play a game which will help us get to know one another. Now form pairs and spend 5 minutes asking questions of your partner. Then swop round. Then form back into the large group, and as if you were your partner, tell the group about yourself, name, background, job plans etc.".

This is typical of the "ice-breaker exercise" - the opening missile in the armoury of the social-skills games player. And it works. Further along the way, the "trust games" involving touching, lifting, leading a temporarily blind person etc. are all used to strengthen the togetherness of the group members. Finally there is learning about 'self' through small group discussion (charade games are used as a now standard technique). We always suspected that although these skill methods were included as the 'meat' of many in-service training courses for those working full or part-time with young people, they were rarely used in the face-to-face situation with youngsters.

Certainly, this has been true of the typical - whatever that is, youth club or centre. Similarly the accent on casework and one-to-one working in many probation and social work departments prevented the easy assimilation of these techniques into practice.

However, the selling of group work has been successful if patchily implemented throughout Britain and the accent of practice in the late 70's is more in tune with the use of games of the relationship or self-awareness type. Adolescent groups have been in some cases bombarded with the whole range of gaming statutory instruments, from getting-to-know-you exercises through the Michael Miles 'Yes/No' game and others right up to the 'heavy end' of the Truth Game and similar which explore group members' weaknesses and strengths. Brain-storming, the method whereby quick-fire answers and suggestions are given to any particular problem is another favourite method used by the games practitioners, in any of the work situations which are thought to require a measure of acceptably administered social education. Games of the style so far mentioned have been much used by workers, because they have correctly realised the potential of the group's shared experience through these techniques. They bring out inhibitions, aggression and provide the framework for gaining confidence. The loner may learn the social skill of speaking in the group through the vehicle of the game, likewise the extrovert bully may be cut to size and forced to evaluate his or her true worth by group pressure.

Certainly, adults using the methods which we include in sections 2 and 4 have often felt even more threatened and vulnerable than the kids. This is another aspect inherent in small group games of this type. Those with the highest and most rigid barriers have the most to lose and ultimately the most to gain through the shared learning experience. In this way, we are already hinting at the level of perception and planning which is necessary on the adults' part. A failing which has often been noticed is that the worker has regarded collections of games as a ready recipe for success. The subsequent games session in the group has then horribly misfired. Rejection and emotional hurt has resulted without the support and care which must be a central part of the process. The going **will** get tough in a group process where a member is told to name another person and the points they like and dislike about them and why (i.e. the Truth Game) to the satisfaction of the entire group. The value of such intensive experiences can be tremendous. Insecure group members may for the first time in their lives, feel the support and warmth of the other group members. They may in the process learn things about themselves and about one another which are personally unique. On a number of occasions we have seen adults and young people who come away from sessions saying: "I've never even told my

4

girl-friend things that I've told the group today." So, the use of different games should be carefully staged to run alongside the natural development of the group. In Intermediate Treatment work this acknowledgement of planning, preparation and support/supervision in games use is now inbuilt into the system of group work practice and no technique is used without some understanding of the possible pitfalls which may be encountered en route and the likely eventual benefits to the group - including the residual frustrations which have to be expected and dealt with accordingly.

Role-playing - the mock interview - the court session - the management committee meeting and others, are all a part of the group work strategies which can be employed to transmit an understanding of self and others' behaviour. The role play is vastly different from the social studies lesson, however. It is not, one hopes (!) stodgy or removed from the young persons' real world of day to day experiences. What it can do, when the process is working well, is to enable the participant to take an observer's view of their own behaviour. It can be a bit like stepping out of the flesh and blood body and externally viewing that body fumbling on through normal existence. If the phrase 'raising consciousness' has any meaning at all it admirably fits the aim these practices are hoped to achieve. Ideally the group members come away from the end of a planned programme of these sessions with a greater understanding of themselves, their peers, the relationship with the other generations, the mechanisms of society and the interface between all these parts. This grandiose claim is obviously far too all encompassing. The experience may be of youngsters opting out of participating, temper tantrums and explosive mixes of personalities within groups. All these shortcomings are inevitable and indeed are closely allied with the nature of the learning experience. Relationship techniques are not going to radicalise society or its members, but in a few cases, individuals may be helped towards coping better with their own selves and those around them.

OTHER GAMES.

That brief description of some of the strengths and weaknesses of the social awareness style of game out the way, we would now like to explain why that part of this production is quite extensive, **BUT** only a relatively small part of the whole.

We feel that it is important to use games, or perhaps more properly 'mechanisms', which allow for the personal development of members of structured groups and in informal situations. What we would wish to add is a debunking of the related myth that **these are the only methods which are professionally viable for aiding the development of relationships and promoting self-awareness.** The arrogance of the relationship gamers is directly analogous with many other groups of workers and academics who wish to develop a core theory and practice body of knowledge; have it legitimised and then protect its validity against all counterfeits. Our view is that any technique which (1) aids adult/youth relationships can lead to (2) a greater personal understanding and (3) a perception of group dynamics and (4) (in some cases) an ability to understand what society in the local and universal sense is about. In a perfect world, (5) is a stage where strategies are developed to cope with the structure and possibly evince changes. Our own situations of working with groups of youngsters may approximate to a far more concrete facet of realism. Take for example Joe and Sandra on the battered, decaying urban housing estate who may have to be helped through their relationship by an adult or group of adults to a position where they no longer refuse to communicate with and distrust all adults, and perhaps are brought a step nearer 'coping behaviour' (a two-way model of them being able to cope with their neighbourhood and vice versa). This could mean thinking twice about nicking every item that 'walks' or a measure of considered stealing - whereby only 'outsiders' get ripped-off rather than everyone, at this stage of their personal development. For workers with youth, this is the experience which, even when its not approved of, may mark a gradual transition of behaviour, from, in Society's eyes, the unacceptable to the acceptable. To aid and abet this modification of behaviour the worker uses the strength of the **personal relationship** which can be formed with individual youngsters. Our contention in this collection, is that almost any game or puzzle, whether ascribed with a social education value or not, can have a positive function in the gaining of a meaningful relationship. In fact, since the setting in which relationship games can be played is limited to the structured group, there is a very real sense of truth in our original sarcastic remark concerning workers learning a range of work methods on training courses and then not being able to practice them in the actual places of work with young people. Finally, if any spelling out is needed of the method, we would remind games users that **enjoyment** need not be a dirty word. Often the best shared experience in the games setting is the result of both parties, adult and youngsters getting a kick out of the task and the related interaction. Success can be measured in terms of young people's willingness to participate and the level to which this involvement allows for future strengthening of adult/ youth relations.

In the choosing of all the games, techniques and simulations included, we have endeavoured to 'humanise' the descriptions by adding our comments on the use of the games, the possible problems thrown up and the type of situation in which they have worked for us. We have not involved ourselves much in the games theory of whether or not one should use 'competitive games', and what possible harmful spin-offs there are. In many ways we find ourselves after testing the various methods with the kids from the Canongate Youth Project and others, supportive of competition, since youngsters have been able to associate more freely with the fun element. Remember, that winning and losing are parts of the Society's rules, which we are concerned with teaching about.

Many adults have forgotten how to play. This is not meant as an insult, rather it is stating the obvious. The puzzles and two player games included in section three are aimed at re-learning on the part of the adult. There is nothing so terribly new about the inclusions, but we have found that the - "Oh yes, I remember that!" reaction from adults is informative in itself. Puzzles when used carefully, i.e. not all in one go, can provide an initial form of contact with youngsters, when the opening gambit of going and having a chat would fail. The other value of the puzzle is that the knowledge can be taken away and tried somewhere else with parents or peers. It can give an insecure youngster a simple skill and a small degree of confidence. It is also fun! The setting in which these, the lateral thinking problems and the paper and pencil, coin and matchstick games can be played is also more flexible than for the more elaborate or structured group games and ethnic and commercial games which require more equipment. Workers often talk about residential experiences being marvellous for developing relationships. So are games, but how many workers, firstly know the rules and secondly are prepared to give the time and effort to personally involve themselves in playing with the youngsters? It is through **participating** that the relationship develops. Later can come the value of a kid being able to teach his or her friends the new game. Returning to the subject of residential work and trips, we have found that many games of all types can be a godsend when the boredom of a long mini-bus trip or a wet weekend in Wales is beginning to take its toll. One seemingly well-known card game injected in the right place can turn a disaster into a success story.

What we have called ethnic games are the pretty normal range of equipment available in many youth work settings. Our question posed at the beginning of our practical tests, was again, how far do workers play with kids using the equipment? From this we obviously received a mixed response, but we noted that only the 'standard' games tended to be played on any given piece of equipment. Both kids and workers we met, were, by and large pretty conservative, but not, happily, opposed to variety and change. 'Other Games' for the dart board, pool table and dominoes are included, as are examples of games such as fives which almost every girl knew as a six year old, only to unlearn with oncoming adolescence. We were amazed by a fifteen year old who sat contentedly displaying her forgotten talents for most of a two hour session.

'New Games' aren't particularly original, but it is a name coined by an American group who have been successfully organising games events for large groups of youngsters and adults. Most involve a high level of physical contact, some trust, and are excellent for using up youthful exuberance and excess energy. The bundle of laughing, yelping, entwined bodies at the end of 'Knots' is a good example. Some team games and outdoor games that have been tried and tested with smaller groups are included in the Activity Games, section 7, but we have made no attempt for this to be a comprehensive selection. Board games of the commercial type are the heritage of most youth groups, but workers could be criticised for only acting as a professional equipment loan service, rarely getting involved with the kids as active group members. Rule books are daunting for most youngsters, therefore it is up to adults to learn the rules, teach them to the kids and actively participate. Longer "Waddington-type" games we found un-acceptable except for the perennial 'Monopoly' and 'Cluedo'. A range of shorter games like 'Baffle Box', and 'Othello' we found entertaining and involving. 'Scrabble' continues to 'work' with a wide range of youngsters and has all the accompanying literacy spin offs. All the games which require score-keeping have numeracy value without appearing to be a disguised maths lesson. Other comments on the usage are included in the descriptions of the individual games.

The use of simulations with youth groups seems to have spawned the greatest quantity of 'learned' writings. We are still unconvinced by either the arguments of these authorities or the practical example of simulation use with the more difficult types of youngsters encountered in Intermediate Treatment work as a general principle. This could easily be our failing, but in general, simulations strike us as being overly long for the sort of kids with whom we are involved and far too complicated, often requiring long periods of setting-up and role determination prior to the period of gaming. The sort of local conflict, Council v Tenants or whatever can be modified to individual settings and be used where structured group settings of youngsters are available. We include references to model examples in the bibliography. In Section Eight, we use 3 models of tried and tested simulations for use in staff sessions and possibly in Senior Member Training. These tend to be a-long-time in the playing and need a debriefing at the end of the session. Star Power is well-known, eventful and in retrospect always produces examples of interesting and noteworthy behaviour. The Tower Game is the most competitive simulation we have come across. It's meant to be so, and gives the group a task to perform with a rigidly defined set of profit targets, based on speed, use of materials and the height of tower built. There is also a whole section on incentives for accurate forward planning.

The Highland Survival concerns the real-life problem of 4 kids, ill-prepared for a hike in the Cairngorms. When the going gets rough, they are confronted with a range of choices. It's an interesting game and an almost believable simulation. These simulations can be successfully used in a one-off course/ conference/staff training session and except with advanced groups of youngsters, we would not see these simulations being used with young people.

We hope that you find the collection useful. We enjoyed collating, producing and testing (playing with) the material. Remember our comment about games being primarily about involvement and the shared fun which should result from their use! Always plan your games sessions with kids, unless it is games of the flexible type which can readily be used in a variety of situations, then you must make sure you have done your homework and learnt the rules! Enjoy yourselves and let us know if you have any games you use and find useful. Also, if you feel we have blundered, we had better know about that as well!

DEBRIEFING AND SENSITIVITY

We would like to stress at this introductory stage in the book that Sections 2 and 4 need to be HANDLED WITH EXTREME CAUTION. These games can trigger off adverse reactions in some disturbed children, and it is necessary for adults, acting in a professional capacity, to have the knowledge to recognise what is happening to the individual in the playing of games where intense emotional feelings are involved.

Debriefing in the end part of a session with kids needs to be sensitively and carefully handled. Professional workers will not leave emotions floating "in the air"; they will work with individuals who are feeling the strain of the sequence or game and aid them to cool off. This is absolutely imperative. Adults must never leave aggression, emotional hurt and tension to drift on outside of a group experience. Ignorance of this proviso could prove fatal!

2 group games icebreakers

GROUP GAMES

(see note on page 10 before using this section).

RELATIONSHIP GAMES

There are various factors involved in the playing of relationship games with groups of young people which have led us to the view that such games should ideally be played in the context of an ongoing programme of social groupwork. Some of these are related to group processes like scapegoating and point to the need for adequate "debriefing" during or after games sessions and for opportunities for individuals to test out skills learnt through games play in other settings like discussions and decision-making forums. Others relate to the unique characteristics of relationship games in as much as they have the potential to promote personal growth and development by enhancing and accelerating normal group processes.

They are qualitatively different from the games discussed elsewhere in the book. Although there may be a high gaming or fun element in them, their use with a group of young people is intended to help individuals acquire the skills which will enable them to communicate and relate better to others. The use of a particular game may be intended to increase self-confidence, encourage constructive criticism of self and others, or foster self-awareness.

All the games have an element of individual risk-taking in them; this might involve physical contact with peers and adults, miming in front of the group, or making personal statements about a group member. Clearly, the major task of the worker(s) is to ensure that there is enough mutual trust and confidence in the group to enable individuals to take such risks without feeling unduly threatened. This is done principally by matching the particular qualities of a game to the stage of development of the group, and by ensuring that adult members of the group "play the game" by participating fully and honestly, thereby putting themselves on an equal footing with other group members in terms of risk-taking and personal vulnerability. Without this quality of commitment to the games from adults, the group is likely to become disillusioned and slip (quite rightly!) into an "us and them" stance.

13

The use of relationship games, then, requires the worker to have some knowledge of group processes and to spend time preparing for sessions. The working through of feelings generated by the games should also be planned for. In the advanced version of the "COMPUTER" game for example, a player may have to read aloud a card which states that he is "THE PERSON WHO HURTS OTHER PEOPLE'S FEELINGS MOST OFTEN". Feelings generated in this kind of game cannot be left hanging in the air, they might therefore be discussed during the game itself, immediately afterwards, or in a separate discussion setting.

Relationship games will work best when there has been adequate preparation of workers and young people, and where some thought has been given to the setting in which the games will be played.

The participation of workers in the games is essential and establishes the norm that each group member should be involved. Older adolescents, in particular, can often be encouraged to play on the grounds that adults will be participating on exactly the same basis as they are.

The introduction of a new game to the group will usually be done by a worker and does not normally imply the possession of any particular skills other than the ability to generate enthusiasm for the game and to explain it lucidly. It does help, though, if the worker has had experience of playing the game, and it is sensible to organise some kind of training session where workers can participate in playing and introducing. This will also serve to familiarise adults with some aspects of the games that they may find initially threatening. Experience of this kind will help adults build up a repertoire of skills that will help them to share the tasks of introducing and organising games. Eventually, this can be shared with young people in the group when they have gained experience of playing particular games.

Relationship games are easier to introduce in an established group where members have built up a degree of trust and confidence in each other, than in a newly established one. Even so, it is important to introduce the games gradually, beginning with "ice-breakers" and physical trust games which will give the group a taste of what is to come while at the same time providing an enjoyable, shared experience. Use of these simple games and techniques will enable workers to ascertain the group's readiness for a move onto the more challenging games and will also help to identify those youngsters who may need extra adult support in this situation. The use of ice-breakers and other introductory techniques can be extended over many sessions with a newly established group until the workers are confident that sufficient group cohesion and trust has been built up. The use of these introductory games themselves contributes significantly to this process.

The playing of relationship games is very much a private group experience and young people cannot therefore be expected to "lay themselves on the line" in a situation where there are constant interruptions or where non-group members are likely to be watching them. Any space used should be large enough to allow for the moving about that some of the games call for, and also for a circle of chairs. Some of the games work better with small numbers (8-10), and a large group (15+) may have to be split up on occasions.

These games can be successfully used with a wide range of young people, although the greatest benefit will be experienced by those who are under stimulated and/or lacking in self-esteem and confidence. In working with this kind of group it should be remembered that young people experiencing this kind of difficulty will present it in a variety of ways; one may be aggressive and challenging with adults and peers, while another may be quiet and withdrawn. Wherever possible, workers should take the opportunity of planning group membership to ensure a balance of personal qualities and social skills. This will tend to create a potentially lively group which can make good use of relationship games and other groupwork techniques.

The introduction of relationship games should pose no great difficulty to those workers already engaged in groupwork with young people, as the skills required are related more to the group worker role than to that of a games specialist.

ICEBREAKERS: NOTES

Our selection of the particular games and sequences in this section is a personal one. **We** would use them heavily in the introductory sessions, but would also use many of them throughout the life of a group.

15

Workers and kids should select games that they are comfortable with - especially in introductory sessions, and should not treat Icebreakers and the Heavy End as mutually exclusive categories.

Brief notes on the planning of games sessions are included, and these, together with our comments on individual games, sequences and exercises are intended to stimulate an awareness in the reader of both the adaptability of relationship games and their complexity.

It is hoped that many of the process issues raised in this section, and the Heavy End, can be read in conjunction with the other sections.

Playing times are offered for rough guidance only - we have known some games, e.g. Truth, Double Dare, to last for hours - others can "burn out" in minutes with some groups. As a general rule of thumb, try to wind games up while there is still interest and enjoyment around - groups will tend to want to repeat positive experiences and will build up a repertoire of games which are important and enjoyable to them.

THE BALL GAME

This is a good way to help a group memorise each others' names quickly. It can be used with any age group, and is more fun with large numbers. The game leader asks the group to stand in a circle and explains that the football he has in his hands is going to help the group memorise each others' names quickly. He states the rules of the game which are simply that when the football is thrown to someone, they catch it, say their own name out loud and then throw the ball to any other member of the group, who must then say their own name and throw the ball on to someone else.

The game benefits from being played at a fast pace, and the leader will therefore encourage this. Once a good rhythm and pace have been set up, the leader will allow this to continue for several minutes, until he feels that people have had a chance to familiarise themselves with each others' names. At this point he will stop the game and introduce a rule change. This calls for people to state the name of the person they are going to throw the ball to, prior to throwing it. The leader will then ask the person holding the ball to continue the game under the new rule.

Further rule changes can be introduced, e.g. not allowing any person to pass the ball twice to the same person, or only allowing passes to people of the opposite sex. Prior to introducing some of these more difficult rules, the group's memory can always be refreshed by playing a few rounds of the original Ball game. Playing time: 10-20 minutes. Can be used in an initial session with the "Hello Game" and "Criss-Cross Naming."

HELLO GAME

This introductory game is especially useful for groups who are meeting together for the first time, and can be used with any age group. The game will work best with a largish group.

You will need a set of prepared action cards which name people in the group. A card might say "Blow a kiss to Mary" or "Shake your fist at Bill". It is important that cards are made up for each person in the group, and this necessitates knowing who will be coming along to the session. Cards will have to be removed for anyone who does not turn up. It is usual in this kind of game to play two or three rounds, giving each person two or three opportunities to pick a card. About 30-45 cards would therefore have to be made up for a 15 strong group. In this case the game would last around 20 minutes - half an hour.

The game is played with everyone sitting in a circle and the leader will then explain that the aim of the game is to help people get to know each other's names. The pile of cards can be placed in the centre of the circle, or can be held by a member of the group. This will be decided by the game leader who might encourage a withdrawn youngster to play by asking him to hand out the cards. The game leader asks for a volunteer to pick the first card, read it out and perform the action. The first volunteer, (probably an adult), will show initial confusion at not knowing who Mary is; it can be overcome by, e.g. asking the person next to him if Mary is the one with the red or black hair, or by addressing all the girls in the group until he finds Mary.

This is a co-operative game, and the leader should encourage players to offer advice to each other and set this example himself. Can be used in an initial session along with "The Ball Game" and "Criss Cross Naming".

SHOUT

This is a good co-operative experience which requires some concentration to work properly. It can be used with any age group and with both large and small groups. The group can be either standing or sitting in a circle.

The leader requires a volunteer to act as "cheerleader", and points out that this person will have to choose a word and whisper it to the group, who will whisper it back. The cheerleader then says the word again, but slightly louder this time, and again it is repeated by the group in unison. The sequence continues until people are yelling as loud as they can.

The role of the cheerleader is very important, as the sequence works best if it builds up gradually to a crescendo. It is often a good idea for an adult to demonstrate this, by volunteering to be "cheerleader".

The sequence can be made more sophisticated by reversing it when the crescendo has been reached, so that the "shouts" become quieter and quieter until they can hardly be heard. Once the group are acquainted with the full sequence a variation can be played where the cheerleader operates a "volume control". In this case the cheerleader controls the volume non-verbally by signalling to the group whether he wants more or less volume. A suitable method of signalling should be demonstrated by the games leader.

Playing time will depend on the number of people who want to try being a cheerleader; it is rarely the case that everyone wants to, and adults in the group should be prepared to encourage people to have a go. With this kind of repetitive sequence it is best to limit the time spent on it to a maximum of 10-15 minutes. "Shout" can be used as a lively introduction to completely different sequences like the "Word Association game" or "Buzz".

TOUCH

This sequence can be used to introduce physical contact to the group. It uses the same clapping rhythm as the "Word Association Game" and can be followed by it quite easily or by one of the physical trust games, like "Passing the Person". The sequence can be used with most age groups but is best suited to largish group.

The clapping rhythm is very important and the leader should ask the group to practice this first, perhaps before explaining the rest of the game. Try a clap-clap-space rhythm, and explain to the group that in the spaces, group members have to touch the person on their left, and then on their right alternatively.

Once this rhythm has been successfully established for a few mintues, the leader can stop the sequence and explain that a different bit of the body must be touched each time - head, toe, arm, hand, etc. The game should be stopped when the group has run out of suitable bits of body! Playing time about 5-10 minutes.

BUZZ

A diabolically simple game in concept, Buzz brings out the mathematical skill in the unlikeliest of people. It can be used with most age groups in a large or small group format. There are a couple of variations - the basic sequence can be used as a quick "taster" before moving on to the others.

The game is played sitting in a circle. The leader explains that it involves counting in turn around the circle e.g. 1, 2, 3, 4, 5, etc, except that the word BUZZ is substituted for the number 7, or multiple of 7 (14, 21, 28 etc), or a number with a 7 in it (e.g. 17, 71, 72 etc). The leader must nominate someone to begin the sequence, by asking her to start with any number between 3 and 6, the numbering going clockwise. So the sequence might go 5, 6, BUZZ, 8, 9, 10, 11, 12, 13, BUZZ, 15, 16, BUZZ, 18, 19, 20, BUZZ, etc.

Once the group have got the hang of this, the leader can introduce a new rule - the direction of numbering round the circle will change at each BUZZ, thus livening up the game considerably! The game can be played where players are out if they make a mistake but this can often lead to most people being out within a couple of minutes! It can often be worthwhile playing several quick rounds without this rule, to build up the group's collective skill, before bringing in elimination.

A further variation involves adding FIZZ (multiples of 5 and numbers with a 5 in them) to BUZZ. So a round might go: 4, FIZZ, 6, BUZZ, 8, 9, FIZZ, 11, 12, 13, BUZZ, FIZZ, 16, BUZZ, 18, 19, FIZZ, BUZZ, etc. 35 because it includes a multiple of 5 and 7 is "FIZZ BUZZ".

Allow about 20 minutes or so.

PASS THE SQUEEZE

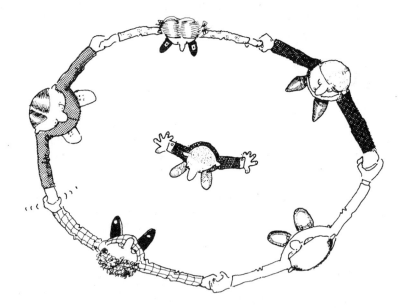

A guessing game which can be used along with similar ones like "Guess the Leader". It can be played with most age groups and works best with largish numbers. Usually played standing (or sitting) in a circle, the aim of the game is for the person in the middle to guess where the squeeze is.

The leader should ask a volunteer to stand in the centre of the circle and ask the rest of the group to hold hands. The leader should explain how the squeeze is passed round the circle i.e. if someone's left hand is squeezed, then that person squeezes the hand he is holding in his right and so on round the circle. It is often worthwhile having a couple of "dry" runs, so that the group get the idea - try asking the group to pass the squeeze as quickly as possible. The squeeze commences with the volunteer turning his back to the person nominated by leader to pass the squeeze. This person can now pass the squeeze to his left or right. The volunteer should be told to shout (Stop!) when he thinks he knows where the squeeze is. Immediately after shouting 'Stop!', the person in the middle must name the person he thinks has the squeeze. If the guess is correct, the two swap places, the person with the squeeze becoming the new person in the middle and the other starting off the new sequence. If the guess is incorrect, the person in the middle should be allowed two more guesses before being replaced by another volunteer.

To keep the sequence going at a brisk pace, the leader should encourage people in the middle to use their guesses fairly quickly, and should discourage group members from stopping the squeeze on its journey round the circle (perhaps to fool the person in the middle, or even just for the hell of it). Allow 20 minutes or so playing time.

RING ON A STRING

A guessing game which is best played in a large group. The leader will need to make sure they have to hand a large loop of string with a ring on it. The loop of string should be big enough to be held by players behind their backs, when they are standing in a circle formation.

A volunteer is required, whose job it is to stand in the middle of the circle and guess where the ring is. The ring, of course, is passed from person to person around the circle behind backs. The leader should stress that the group needs to "fox" the person in the middle by keeping their hands moving and faking passes of the ring. When the volunteer thinks he knows where the ring is, he should shout 'stop', and make his guess. If he is correct, he swaps places with the holder of the ring, who becomes the next person in the middle.

To start the game off, the leader should ask the volunteer to face away from a nominated person who will start the ring on its way round the circle. The leader must decide on the number of guesses allowed - three is a good number the first time the game is played; experienced groups can be limited to one. If a person's guesses are all incorrect, the leader will have to nominate someone in the middle or ask for a volunteer. Some youngsters (and adults too) may have genuine difficulty in working out where the ring is - in this situation the leader should strongly encourage guessing, to prevent possible embarrassment to the person in the middle and to maintain the pace of the sequence.

Playing time should be limited to a maximum of 15-20 minutes. "Ring on a String" can be played as an enjoyable set with other guessing games e.g. "Guess the Leader", "Who Am I?".

KILLER

A very popular trust game with plenty of opportunity for amateur dramatics! This game is best suited to a large group of teenagers, and is played sitting in a circle. A little advance preparation is required, as one "Killer" must be randomly chosen for each round of the game. This can be done by passing a piece of paper to each group member, with a cross on one piece, denoting the killer. Alternatively, the person introducing the game can use playing cards, one for each member of the group, denoting, say, the Ace of Spades as the killer card.

Players should be instructed to look individually at their card or piece of paper, without letting anyone else see it.

The stage is now set - there is a killer in the room, but no-one (except the killer) knows who it is. The killer kills by winking so make sure that there is opportunity for good eye contact between group members. The rules of the game are quite simple:-

1. The killer tries to kill as many people as possible before being discovered. He kills by looking directly at someone, and winking once.
2. Anyone on the receiving end of a wink is dead, and out of the game, but must wait a few seconds before "dying" dramatically. This is a crucial rule and must be strictly adhered to, as it increases the killer's chances of remaining undetected and therefore tends to prolong the game into its more exciting stages where people are dropping like flies and panic begins to set in.

3. Anyone, at any time, can make a guess at the killer's identity. If the guess is correct, the killer must own up, and a new round begins. If the guess is incorrect, the person who made it must die (dramatically if possible) and the game continues.

Killer is a good shared experience and helps build confidence in individuals. Considerable status can be obtained by being a good killer. Allow 20-30 minutes.

WORD ASSOCIATION GAME

This sequence can get people working together really well as a group, and is great fun to play, especially with large numbers.

The game puts people "on the spot" in a mock-threatening way, and by its insistence on equal participation from all, helps to build up confidence in individual group members.

The leader should get the group to sit in a circle and practice a clapping rhythm, e.g. clap-clap-space, before explaining that in the spaces people have to say out loud around the circle a word connected to the one that has just been said by their neighbour.

A volunteer is needed to say the first word, with the person on, say, the right then having to give a related word. So a round might go clap-clap-house-clap-clap-garden-clap-clap-hose-clap-clap-water etc.

Once the group have got used to the sequence, it can be played with the stipulation that anyone who fails to get their word in before the "clap-clap-" sounds again is out. It is also possible to challenge players if e.g. someone thinks that a word does not have an association with the previous one. Other rules can be added, like not allowing a word to be repeated in any one round, or not at all.

It is usual to play several rounds of the basic sequence before tightening up on the chosen rules and playing it on a competitive basis. Watch out for words like xx! or xxx!! slipping in to test out adults' personal boundaries. The Word Association Game can be played for up to 25-30 minutes.

PASSING ON OBJECTS

This is a simple miming sequence which can be used with any age group to encourage imaginative responses to mime situations. Any number can participate, but it should be noted that adult involvement is crucial in providing a variety of miming models which youngsters can copy and adapt. It is advisable, therefore, to use this sequence with large inexperienced groups only when there are several adults around to participate and offer encouragement and guidance to other players.

The basic technique involves the group sitting in a circle and passing an imaginary object to each other round the circle. The sequence will start with the games leader herself, or someone nominated by her . Good objects to pass are things like; sticky chewing gum, a heavy rock, a pet rabbit, etc. Try to make sure that the person starting the sequence off is able to mime imaginatively and can encourage their neighbour to accept the object in a way appropriate to the mime. This process can be helped by other adults in the group, who should feel free to encourage the group to "tune in" to the mime by commenting, "What is it? - it must be something really sticky" or "I wouldn't like to have **that** passed to me in the dark!".

Each object should pass completely round the circle before the leader asks for another volunteer or nominates someone to start off a new object. When using the basic technique, the objects should be "known" either by the leader stating that e.g. a heavy rock is about to be passed round the group, or by the person starting the sequence, picking a card and reading it out. A prepared set of 5 or 6 cards should be enough before moving on to other variations.

The first one involves asking the group not just to pass the imaginary object, but to do this while pretending to be a particular kind of person, e.g. "policemen, old lady, social worker, delinquent, etc." So the whole group could act as e.g. old ladies, or individuals could be selected to role play different characters, perhaps by distributing prepared cards with a character on each one.

The second variation involves each person changing the object received into something else before passing it on. So someone might receive a piece of sticky chewing gum and "mould" it into a

24

teapot before passing it on. Again, adult involvement is important in encouraging the group to work out what each new object is, and perhaps whether the mime could have been more helpful by being done in a different way.

While the basic sequence is fairly simple, the variations are quite demanding and should be gradually introduced to the group over several sessions. About 15-20 minutes should be allowed for each sequence. They can be used as a good introduction to "Clay Modelling" or "People".

PEOPLE

Basically a "silly" game, it nonetheless introduces the group to the idea of labelling individuals with particular attributes. It can also involve some spontaneous miming and is probably best used with a large group of under 15's.

A set of funny "people" cards is required, one for each person in the group. Cards will be along the lines of "Kermit", "Hot Lips", "Tarzan" etc. The leader will start the game by nominating someone to take a card from the pile and asking them to give it to the person he thinks it suits best! - without saying what is on the card. That person keeps the card, chooses one himself and gives it to the most appropriate person, and so on until each person has **one card only.**

The leader now asks the group to introduce themselves to each other, starting with the person who took the first card, who might give a typical Tarzan yodel and say "I'm Tarzan". The sequence continues around the circle until everyone has introduced themselves. The leader can suggest doing the introductions again, but this time with some mime appropriate to each character. Playing time: about 20 minutes.

GET KNOTTED!

Although essentially a small group physical experience, this game has great spectator value, so it can easily be played by different combinations of 6 or 8 people from a larger group.

This is one of many contact experiences which help young people of all ages get used to the idea of physical touch and expression. In a small group situation, the leader would be expected to participate in the experience with the whole group but this is not crucial in a larger group where the leader can occupy a "director-type" role.

The sequence requires one of the 6-8 players to leave the room or turn away while the rest "Get knotted". They do this by standing in a circle holding hands and then tangling themselves up by (still holding hands!) crawling between legs, stepping over linked arms, etc. When they are well and truly knotted, the remaining player attempts to untie them without using violence and with the others still holding hands.

The sequence can be repeated several times and may last for 15 minutes or so. Contact experiences like this one can be used together as a series to finish off a session in an enjoyable way.

ESCAPE/OUTSIDER

This is a good rough and tumble contact exercise for most ages, which is best used with largishgroups. There are several variations which involve a volunteer breaking into, or out of a circle formed by the rest of the group.

Considerable frustration can be experienced by the volunteer, who must pit himself against the collective strength of the group as they try to contain or exclude him. The sequence can therefore be used to stimulate discussion around the areas of frustration and alienation.

If the exercises are to be used as a lead-in to discussion, this should be stated by the leader who should ask the group to concentrate on their feelings as they go through the exercises. Discussion can focus on questions like "How would you describe your behaviour during the various exercises?", "Which exercises did you like/dislike the most, and why?" "What feelings did you have for people in the group as you went through the exercises?".

The basic sequence begins with the group standing in a circle with linked arms, and the volunteer on his own in the middle. The leader should explain the purpose of the exercise, namely that the group have to stop the volunteer breaking out of the circle without using violence. They must keep arms linked at all times but are otherwise free to move around and bunch together to keep the volunteer contained in the circle. Most people will in fact, manage to break out of the circle, but it is a useful precaution to have something like a 90 second limit for each volunteer - this also helps to set a brisk pace for the exercises.

When the person has successfully broken out, or the time limit has expired, a new volunteer can take his place in the centre of the circle. This initial sequence can be repeated several times, or can be alternated with the variations, the first of which involves the volunteer **outside the circle** trying to break into it. The group, who have their backs to the "Outsider", are therefore in the position of ignoring him.

A second variation involves the group facing outwards (still with linked arms) towards the outsider who again has to try and break into the circle.

The leader should ensure, that as far as possible, all group members have a chance to experience the outsider role. The leader will find a 'neutral' approach useful, which will allow space for offers of advice to the group about blocking ploys as well as to the outsider about techniques for breaking through the circle. Obviously all variations need not be used in one session. Allow about ½ an hour for the sequences and another ½ hour for any discussion that is required.

ARMADILLO

Confusion is the end result of this sequence and is perfectly in order, as "Armadillo" comes into the category of "silly" games! Although it can be played in the small group setting, it is tremendous fun in a large group.

"Armadillo" is a passing sequence, so the person introducing the game should be equipped with a small object like a pen or pencil and ensure that the players are seated in a circle. The sequence goes like this:-

The person nominated to start the sequence (Player 1) takes the pen and passes it to the person on his right, saying "This is an armadillo!". Player 2 asks Player 1 "What is it?" and Player 1 repeats "It's an armadillo". Player 2 now passes the pen to the person on his right (Player 3), saying "This is an armadillo!". Player 3 asks Player 2 "What is it?", Player 2 then asks Player 1 "What is it?", and Player 1 states to player 2 **"It's an Armadillo!"**. Player 2 states to player 3, "It's an Armadillo!", thus giving Player 2 a reply to his question. Player 3 can now pass the pen to Player 4, stating "This is an Armadillo!".

If you have read this carefully (and have an I.Q. of 140!) you'll have worked out that when a player receives the pen, his question "What is it?" must be repeated anti-clockwise around the group until it reaches Player 1, whose reply "It's an armadillo!" must pass clockwise all the way back to the player with the pen before he can pass it on. Eventually, with a bit of luck, the pen finds its way back to Player 1.

"Armadillo" is a lot easier to play than it is to explain, so give it a try with the group after the minimum of explanation, and give advice to players as the game continues. Once the group have got the hang of it, the full version can be played. This involves Player 1 starting the sequence as before, and then immediately passing another pen or pencil to his left, stating "This is a hippopotamus!". There's a fair chance that when the objects meet, the sequence will collapse in jovial confusion!

Most groups will want to try the sequence again and this should be encouraged but adults should resist any temptation to press the group into "doing it correctly", as the concentration required for this will often come spontaneously, as players become "hooked" by the sequence.

Good for building verbal confidence and aiding concentration. "Armadillo" can often entertain a group for up to half an hour.

POCOMANIA

Like "Armadillo", this is a totally silly sequence which is great fun. It can be used with most groups, provided they are in a silly mood! The group should be standing or sitting in a circle, holding hands. The leader nominates someone to start the sequence by making a **continuous** noise and squeezing the hand of the person on his right who makes a different continuous noise and squeezes the hand of the person on her right who makes another continuous noise, and so on around the circle until everyone is making a noise. At this point, i.e. when the squeeze returns to the person who started the sequence, he stops making his noise and squeezes the hand of the person on his right who stops making her noise and squeezes the hand of the person on her right, and so on round the circle until silence reigns! The sequence can be repeated several times at different speeds, either clockwise or anti-clockwise. Allow 15 minutes or so.

LINK-UP

A guessing game which can be adapted for use with most groups, large and small.

It is often difficult to anticipate how easy or difficult players will find some of the association cards that have to be made up - it's worthwhile making up two or three sets of cards of increasing difficulty which can be used in one session of the game. This avoids being stuck with one large set of cards which turn out to be far too easy for the group. Use a range of words like - home; warm; kind; carrot; evil; lovely; money; steal; pain; child, and make up enough cards to allow each player two or three "goes".

The person introducing the game should ensure that people are sitting comfortably in a circle. A volunteer takes the first card and it is explained that they must look at the word on the card and then say out loud any word that it immediately brings to mind. The rest of the group then have the task of trying to guess what the word on the card is. So if someone picks up a card with "man" on it, they might say "moustache". Other people might then guess "face, hair, prickly" until someone guesses "man". The person who guesses correctly picks up the next card and makes an association, and so on around the group.

Occasionally, people may make rather obscure link-ups which are difficult to guess. In such cases the leader should intervene before players become too frustrated, by asking someone to take another card - perhaps after hearing what the obscure link-up was. With encouragement from adults in the group, the game can be played quite briskly and it usually creates a nice feeling of group achievement. It can be used as a prelude to the "Word Association Game", and lasts for about 10-15 minutes.

CRISS CROSS NAMING

This game calls for the group to be well acquainted with each others' names. It is suitable for any age group and will work best with large numbers. The game is played with the group standing in a circle. The leader explains that this game has to be played pretty fast and that people will have to concentrate quite hard on what they are doing. He will call for, or nominate, someone to start off by calling the name of someone opposite while moving across the circle to take their place. The person named must move off across the circle calling the name of someone else opposite them, before the original person arrives at their place, and so on.

Part of the fun of this kind of game is that it often ends up in confusion! The leader may have to start the group off several times until there is a good rhythm going, which he will allow to continue for several minutes. At this point he will exercise his sadistic tendencies by stopping the game and calling for a rule change which stipulates that two people (and then three) start off the game!

In this kind of sequence, adults should keep tuned in to what the group are getting from it. There is fun to be gained from the confusion and the physical contact when people get tangled up in the middle of the circle, but there can also be considerable shared enjoyment generated by practicing the game until it runs (more or less) smoothly. Playing time: 20 minutes. Criss Cross Naming can be played in an initial session after the "Hello Game" and the "Ball Game".

PASSING THE PERSON

"Passing the Person" is a physical trust sequence best played with a large group of teenagers. The person introducing the sequence must organise the group into two lines of equal numbers facing each other, and about four feet apart. If it is an odd-numbered group, then the "odd man out" can be the first volunteer. With even numbers, the leader should ask for a volunteer, and should not participate in the sequence himself, thus leaving two lines of equal number.

The sequence involves each person crossing arms and holding hands with the person immediately opposite. This forms a chain of hands along which the volunteer can be passed with a rocking motion. He can either take a running jump on to the hands, (not advised for the first time round !), or he can be helped by the first two couples at one end lowering their hands so that he can be supported by them and then raised to the same level as the others, before being passed along the line.

31

Passing the Person can often be played at a cracking pace, as the line of crossed arms provides a very secure support for the person being passed; the difficult bit comes at the end of the pass when the people at the end of the line have to work out how to get the volunteer back on the floor again - simply chucking him off the end of the line is not to be recommended!

An alternative sequence can be used which involves the group standing in a tight circle, and passing the person carefully round it. This is a more difficult trust game and demands a lot of co-operation between group members for the person to be passed smoothly round the circle. As with any trust sequence, all players should have a chance to experience it. They are good co-operative experiences for a group and can often be used to round off sessions nicely. Allow half an hour or more if both sequences are used.

TRUST: BACK TO BACK

Mark Green told us of this one which is used at the Clubbie in Dundee. Best suited to small groups, although its spectator element does give it potential for use with larger numbers.

This is a "Mirror-type" sequence, with similarities to some mime exercises. Two volunteers are required to sit back to back in close physical contact, i.e. with bodies touching from base of the spine to the head. Stools are ideal-chairs with backs impossible - or players can sit on the floor.

The sequence is simplicity itself - Player 1 is asked to move bits of her body in contact with Player 2, e.g. shoulder blades, head etc. Player 2 is instructed to "mirror" these movements. It often helps if the players keep their eyes shut during the sequence. Allow a few minutes, and then reverse the leadership role, by asking Player 2 to lead off.

Back to back trust has a lot of potential, and is undoubtedly capable of variation, e.g. what about all the members of a large group carrying out the exercise simultaneously?

WHO AM I?

This is a very popular guessing game suitable for small and large groups of most ages. Some equipment is needed, namely a large safety pin, and some sheets of paper with the names of famous personalities on them, e.g. "Kermit", "Wonderwoman", "Elvis Presley", etc. The names should be large and clear enough (use a felt marker!) to be easily read at a distance of 6 feet or so. The number of sheets of paper will dictate the length of the game, but allow at least one per player.

The person introducing the game finds someone to go into the middle of the seated circle and explains that that person has to guess the name on the sheet which will shortly be pinned on their back. This is done by asking questions of other people in the group - who can only answer "yes" or "no". Questions should be asked which will narrow down the range of possibilities, and lead towards a solution.

A series of questions might therefore include ones like this: "Is it a famous film star?", "Is it a pop star?", "Is it a male?", "Is he alive?", "Did he live in this country?", "Did he live in America?", "Was he one of these rock'n'roll singers?", "Is it Elvis Presley?" - YES!!

Asking the "correct" questions is quite a skill, and most players will require considerable adult help in developing them. This can be done quite simply by having adults take the first few "goes", therefore offering models for the group to imitate. The game itself can be designed in an easy version, if desired, by taking all the famous personalities from one category e.g. pop stars, cartoon characters, footballers.

Adults should feel free to help people out by suggesting good questions for them to ask, or areas to explore e.g. age, sex, looks, personality, etc.

So the game starts with someone in the middle of the circle having a name pinned on their back and turning completely round a couple of times so that the rest of the group can read the name. The person in the middle then has to ask questions of individuals in the group that will help him work out the name pinned on his back. Group members can only answer "Yes" or "No" to questions put.

The person can guess the name at any point during the round - if correct, someone takes his place and a new round begins. A time limit, or a limitation as to the number of guesses, can be useful in maintaining pace.

If introduced and explained well, this usually turns out to be a really popular game to play. It builds up social confidence and offers a real sense of achievement as members find they can succeed in guessing "Who am I?".

Playing time: 30 minutes or so.

CLAY MODELLING

A contact game which is useful in introducing the group to mime skills, Clay Modelling involves one person moulding two or three others into an object or situation. There is good spectator value in "clay modelling" and it can therefore be played in large and small groups.

It is suitable for most age groups if care is taken to make the range of objects and situations relevant. These should be worked out in advance of the session and transferred to cards - e.g. "Two footballers after scoring a goal," "An armchair", "A pop star", etc. The cards should also state the number of bodies needed to make each scenario.

The leader should ask for a volunteer who would like to be the first modeller. This person picks a card, but does not tell the group what is written on it. He then chooses the number of people stipulated on the card and proceeds to mould the people into a scenario in the middle of the circle.

Many youngsters may need adult help and encouragement to mould the bodies into recognisable objects or situations. The remainder of the group must try to guess what it is. The first person to guess correctly, becomes the next modeller, and so on.

With an inexperienced group, the leader may wish to miss out the guessing component, and concentrate instead on encouraging the group to help the modeller by telling them what object or situation the modeller is attempting to create and asking for suggestions as to how this can best be achieved. If each player has a chance to be the modeller, the game could last for 30 minutes+.

CONSEQUENCES

Most folk will have played consequences at some time in their lives, and it is therefore rare to find a group of young people who can't between them remember the rules of the play. Consequences works well in large and small groups and is enjoyed by most ages.

The person introducing the game must make sure that each player has a piece of paper and a pencil. The game involves players writing down a suitable word or phrase for each item in the following list:

1. An adjective applicable to a girl.
2. A girl's name
3. An adjective applicable to a boy
4. A boy's name

5. Where they met
6. What she did
7. What he did
8. What she said
9. What he said
10. What the consequence was
11. What the world said

The sequence works as follows: The leader nominates someone to to read out the items from the list, one at a time, making sure that players have enough time to think of, and write down their word or phrase. After each word or phrase has been written down, papers should be folded over so that the writing cannot be seen and passed to the person on the right, before the next item is read out, and so on.

When the sequence has been completed, the papers are read out individually starting with someone nominated by the leader. Players should be asked, when reading, to add in any obvious words needed to maintain continuity.

Consequences is an enjoyable shared experience which invariably produces very funny "stories". Often used to round off a session, it takes about 15-20 minutes to complete each full sequence.

LIVING SCULPTURE

This can be a hilarious contact sequence when used spectator fashion although it also works in the small group setting. There are similarities with "Clay modelling", which makes it quite easy to use the two as a set.

The modelling in this case is done in a fairly random manner, resulting in contortions, chaos and laughter.

The person introducing the sequence requires 7 volunteers, one of whom will be the modeller - he is required to sit or stand with his back to the others while they form a standing circle and hold hands. The leader should now number off the people in the circle from 1-6 and ask the modeller to shout out action instructions along the lines of: "No 4 lift up No 1's leg, "No 3 put your arm round No 6's neck", "No 2 crawl through No 4's legs", etc. The groups' hands must remain linked for as long as is humanly possible, and at some point (preferably prior to the collapse of the group in a heap in the middle of the floor!), the modeller should be instructed by the leader to turn round and view the "Living Sculpture" he has created.

Some "modellers" may need help in thinking up appropriate instructions and it is important that adult help is offered if it does not come spontaneously from the group. The sequence can be repeated several times and may last for 20-30 minutes.

YES/NO

The archetypal "catch you out" game. Suitable for large and small groups of most ages. YES/NO must be played fairly fast, if it is to work properly, so the leader should spend time explaining the rules carefully and organising a "dry" run.

The leader must nominate someone (or obtain a volunteer) who is to be first on the spot, and will answer questions from the rest of the group without saying "yes" (or "aye") or 'no'. Questions should be fired at this person as quickly as possible, commencing with the person on his right, and carrying on right round the group. A time limit, of say, 30 seconds should be imposed for each round. If the person answers "yes" or "no" to any question they are immediately out, and are replaced by the person on the left, and so on round the circle.

Anyone completing the 30 seconds should be given a round of applause! The game can be varied - and made much more difficult - by insisting that replies to questions must be lies!

Allow about 20 minutes playing time.

GUESS THE LEADER

The group should be seated in a circle for this game. It's a very popular guessing sequence which is suitable for youngsters of most ages and is best played in a large group.

Two volunteers are required to start the sequence off - one to be the "leader", and another to guess who the leader is. The person who is going to "guess the leader" should be asked to leave the room, while the group choose a leader whose actions they will all copy. These actions can range from hand-clapping and feet-stamping to the more subtle ones like nose-picking and back-scratching! The leader must regularly change the action and the group must copy immediately.

The action sequence should be started before the volunteer is asked to come back into the room. When they do, they should be asked to stand in the middle of the circle and have three guesses at who the leader is. If they guess correctly, then the leader leaves the room, a new person is selected to lead the group, and the sequence can be repeated. If all three guesses are unsuccessful, the same procedure can be followed.

Most groups pick this game up very easily, provided that the actions are changed regularly by the leader - this gives the person in the middle a fair chance and also helps keep the game moving at a good pace. It can be worth reminding the group not to stare directly at the leader all the time, as this makes it ridiculously easy for the person in the middle. Useful for increasing self-confidence it is a good finisher to the end of a session. Playing time about 20 minutes.

TRUST - IN A CIRCLE - THE FEET GAME

This trust sequence is best used as a small group experience with teenagers but it can be used with 8-10 members of a larger group. The games leader should explain the trust concept to the group, taking care to point out the need for everyone's participation for the experience to work properly. She should then ask the group to stand in a fairly tight circle, arms outstretched, with a volunteer in the middle. It is important that the volunteer keeps their arms at their sides, feet together and body rigid. This is no easy matter, but it usually comes after one or two tries and the knowledge that you are not going to land flat on your back!

The sequence commences with the volunteer leaning backwards until he loses balance; he is then "caught" by the outstretched arms of the person immediately behind him and pushed gently back towards the centre of the circle.

As trust is built up between the volunteer and the group, he can be allowed to fall further before being caught, and can be pushed to the centre (or **around** the circle) more energetically.

The leader should take account of the physical size and strength of participants - the sequence will not work with eight average 12 year olds and a 12 stone adult in the middle.

This is particularly important with the more energetic variation "The Feet Game". This is exactly the same sequence - played sitting down! Players should arrange themselves in a circle on the floor with feet outstretched towards the centre and arms raised to catch the (small!) volunteer in the middle!

Trust sequences like this demand that the adults involved are constantly encouraging feedback between group and volunteer, e.g. "What does it feel like, Jim?" "Is it easier now that you know you're not going to fall?" Adult support and encouragement is crucial in presenting the sequence in such a way that even the most timid youngster will be prepared to "have a go". Sequences like these are popular with most groups and are often played two or three at a time to round off an evening's activity. All members of the group should be given the opportunity to experience the sequences. Average playing time for "Trust": 20-30 minutes.

THE MINISTER'S CAT

Only suitable for small groups, this sequence is useful for increasing the self-image of individuals. The group should be seated in a circle, while the leader explains that the objective is for each person in the group to take it in turns to give the minister's cat a different adjective, beginning with the same letter, i.e. "A", "B", "C", and so on through the alphabet. The leader can indicate what is required by giving examples of what people might say for the letter "T", e.g. Bill might say "The minister's cat is a terrible cat", Jean might say "The minister's cat is a tired cat", Irene might say "The minister's cat is a tricky cat", etc.

The sequence starts with the leader nominating someone to give the minister's cat an adjective beginning with the letter "A". At the end of each round (i.e. when everyone in the group has given the cat an adjective beginning with the appropriate letter) the person who started the sequence is first to use the next letter in the alphabet. The sequence can be played right through the alphabet, missing out difficult letters like, "Q", "V", "X", "Y", "Z", etc, or can be limited to a number of rounds e.g. 10.

A variation exists which requires players to give the cat a name as well as an adjective e.g. "The minister's cat is an ancient cat and its name is Alfie", "The minister's cat is an amiable cat and its name is Agnes", etc.

Adults in the group should be ready to offer encouragement to players who are having genuine difficulty in thinking of an appropriate adjective or name.

The sequence should not be used competitively - rather as an opportunity for the group to work together to complete the task successfully. 20 mins+ playing time.

ADVERB GAME

Adults may have to brush up their miming skills for this game, as it involves acting out various attributes, e.g. acting stupidly, happily, sexily etc. The game always benefits from adults giving a lead, and encouraging withdrawn or embarrassed participants to "get into it".

The adverb game is played sitting in a circle, and requires one person to leave the room while an adverb is chosen. The leader can involve the group in choosing an adverb, in which case   having a few good suggestions in mind, just in case people "dry up". Alternatively, a set of prepared cards can be used, with one being drawn at random each time a new adverb is required. The player outside the room has the task of guessing which adverb has been chosen - this is done by deduction from the (hopefully accurate!) acting of the other players. They should be reminded that they must answer questions put to them by acting in the manner of the chosen adverb. So if the adverb is "aggressive", a player might answer a question like "what's the time" by "squaring up" and saying "what's it to you?".

When the group is ready, the leader should ask the person outside to come into the centre of the circle and question individual players, before trying to guess the adverb. As with similar games, players should be encouraged to use their guesses fairly quickly so that the game has good pace. A new volunteer is required to leave the room (and therefore start off a new round) each time someone runs out of guesses, or manages to name the adverb. This game can be used, with others of similar nature, to promote miming and acting skills. Allow about 15 minutes playing time.

WOOLLY TALKING

A superb groupwork tool which can be used to illustrate in a concrete manner, which group member "hogs" the conversation, or who rarely contributes etc. Perfect in the small group setting, Woolly Talking might get out of hand in a large group! Players should be seated in a circle and the person introducing the sequence should equip himself with a large ball of wool! This technique could be used in conjunction with some kind of discussion leader, or simply a "free for all" conversation.

41

As soon as someone speaks, the ball of wool should be passed to them, while the leader retains a firm hold on the loose end. The wool is kept taut, and should be passed on to the next person to speak (or attempt to speak!), while the original contributor maintains a secure hold on his bit of wool.

As the conversation progresses, the space in the centre of the circle will soon be taken up with a criss-cross pattern of wool which will show e.g. who spoke the most/least times, who spoke before or after a particular person, etc.

This technique gives tremendous opportunity to the group to analyse several aspects of their verbal interactions.

PYRAMID

"Pyramid" is an exciting physical experience with some of the characteristics of "Get Knotted!". Very much a spectator event, the action is performed by five members of a large or small group. The nature of the Pyramid challenge forces the five into close physical contact with each other and necessitates a degree of group co-ordination and planning.

The person introducing the game should ask five volunteers to stand in the middle of the seated circle of 'spectators', and explain that they must arrange themselves so that there are only four feet on the ground. This is the basic challenge, which can be varied to stipulate e.g. two feet and two hands on the ground. A time limit of two minutes to complete the task can be used, and it's a good idea to ask the volunteers to hold their Pyramid position for five seconds. If the task isn't completed within the time limit, the volunteers can be given another chance, or can be replaced.

Most kids can work out a solution quite easily, but if they do get into difficulty, adults can encourage the group to offer advice.

There are numerous 'solutions' to Pyramid and this, together with the variables introduced by the physical size of participants, leads to a constantly changing spectator event. Allow 20 minutes playing time with most age groups.

LIAR

Liar can be used with both small and large groups. It falls into the category of 'silly' games, but it is none the less a useful way of developing mime skills.

The sequence is usually played with the group seated in a circle. The rules are quite simple - you have to mime an activity, and lie about it when your neighbour asks what you're doing!

Someone should be nominated to start the sequence. This person must think of an activity and mime it well enough so that everyone knows what he's meant to be doing (e.g. having a shower). While he is miming, his neighbour (on the right, say) must ask "What are you doing?" The first person must lie, so he might say that he's picking his nose, or something like that. The second person must now mime this activity (i.e. picking his nose) and when asked by the person on his right "What are you doing?", he must lie and state that he is doing something completely different, like dribbling a ball. The sequence continues in this way, right round the circle, and can be repeated if required.

It's worthwhile using Liar every now and again, to brush up the group's miming skills. It's a lot of fun to play, and folk usually don't mind being pulled up if their mimes are inadequate.

Liar is suitable for most age groups. Allow 10-20 minutes playing time.

LEVITATION

This trust experience has several variations and it is one of the many sequences where the inter-dependence of group members is illustrated in a practical way. Suitable for all but the youngest groups it can be used as both a small group and "spectator" experience.

The basic technique is very simple, and involves 6 or 8 people offering one another the experience of "levitation". As levitation will only be experienced by one person at a time, the leader should stress the need for making this as enjoyable as possible by allowing the chosen person to relax completely. A calm and quiet atmosphere should be suggested.

Once the leader has assembled the "team", the sequence can begin. The subject should be blindfolded and asked to lie, face upwards, on the floor and relax. It should be stressed to her that the others are going to lift her up and carry her around the room and no way will she be allowed to fall. The aim of the leader and the team is to reassure the subject and allow her to relax completely and enjoy the experience.

Levitation commences with the team lining up in equal numbers on either side of the subject, squatting down and lifting the person very gently from the floor making sure that the head is well supported and the body is horizontal and straight. The team can now stand and transport the subject at different heights and even above their heads without too much difficulty.   ·

Throughout, the leader should be encouraging feedback from the subject as to how they are feeling, how far they think they are off the ground etc. The scenario created for each subject will differ according to the leader's perception of how well they will handle the sequence.

For example, a timid person may have to be given a lot of positive support throughout, while a more robust youngster might be teased by manufacturing a collision with the "roof". In reality the roof would be something like a plank of wood held by a couple of people just above the subject. If most members of a small group are keen to be levitated, then this sequence can last for 30 minutes or more. Levitation can be used along with other trust games e.g. "Passing the Person", "Trust", etc.

I WENT TO MARKET

Sometimes called "I went to the shops", this is a memory game suitable for large and small groups of most ages. The basic idea is that the group builds up a massive shopping list which has to be memorised, added to, and repeated as each player's turn comes round.

The sequence is played sitting in a circle, and begins with a volunteer stating the first item that was bought at the market, e.g. "I

went to market and bought a **shirt**". Thereafter the sequence continues clockwise with each player adding to the list, e.g. "I went to market and bought a shirt and a tie and a lollipop", and so on round the group.

Players are capable of memorising an amazing number of items, once a few rounds have been played. At this point, the sequence can be started anew, with players being ruled out of the game when their memory fails them.

Allow about 20 minutes+ playing time.

HORROR STORY

Definitely not for the squeamish! This shared experience plays on the adolescent's fascination with the supernatural and other generally horrible things and demands a fair degree of improvised story telling skill on the part of one of the adults in the group.

Horror Story should be introduced quite casually to the group and only carried through if the group are 100% keen on hearing it. The story teller will normally ask something like: "Have any of you heard the story about the wee boy who died in this building years and years ago?" Depending on the response, the story teller will continue. His aim of course, is for the group to drag the story out of him, so initially he might say "I don't really know if I should tell you, 'cos its a really horrible story!" When at last the group persuade him to continue, he should insist that the lights are switched out so that the room is plunged into total darkness.

The story could centre round the horrible death, 100 years ago, of a boy who had some connection with the building the group are presently using. A plan for such a story might be:-

The building used to be a bakery, run by a horrible old man with a foul temper; a boy used to work in the bakery, and quite liked it for a while; but things between him and the baker got steadily worse because of the baker's bad temper; one day they had a terrible argument, and the baker knocked him out and flung him into the deep, damp cellar, where he was left to be eaten alive by rats.

Obviously the success of this experience depends very much on the story teller's ability to improvise and embellish the plot. This is not as difficult as it might seem, bearing in mind that the captive audience are likely to be quite enthralled (not to mention terrified) by the incredible story.

A quite dastardly variation on Horror Story is to include in the plot, the dismembering of a body. At this point, various bits of body can be passed round the group - carrots are good for fingers! peeled grapes for eyes etc.

Allow 20 minutes or so, ideally with a largish group.

GAMES SESSIONS: COMMENTS

The following are possible "Starters" as kids arrive:

	Ethnic Games		**Commercial Games**
½ hr	Pool		Scrabble
	Darts	+	Baffle Box
	Cards		Mastermind

The above format is a useful one to start off with, if the group has a suitable base to work from. The lack of such a base need not be a major hurdle to overcome, as all the above games (excepting pool) are easily transportable, and can be set up and used almost anywhere.

We chose the combination of Ethnic and Commercial Games, as they cater for groups as well as one to one interaction. Young people in the group can therefore find themselves involved in several different types of gaming situations in a half hour period e.g. Sandy might have a game of 8 ball pool (doubles) with three other people, moving on to Mastermind - a two player game.

Using games in this context, workers can allow kids who are new to the group experience enough space to make choices about the kind of game they play and the number of people they get involved with at any particular time. Our selection of Ethnic/Commercial games will be known to most young people and this should help allay any uncomfortable feelings which might otherwise be generated in introductory sessions by "pushing" games which are unfamiliar.

Should this kind of opener to an I.T session or a youth club evening become a regular feature, one would expect the inclusion of some unfamiliar games, and an emphasis on encouraging the group to try e.g. Rotation Pool, Shanghai Darts, Switch, Spoons, etc.

Prior to any session involving games, workers would be expected to consider their response to young people who are non-participators. Adults generally find it extremely difficult to understand and work with the (quite common) adolescent

47

response of "I'm not going to play your ****** silly games."

Much will depend on the expectations that kids have of the sessions, and any contracts or agreements they have made with workers.

If, for example, gaming is to be a regular feature of the sessions and kids have "contracted-in" to the group on this understanding, then the response quoted above is clearly unreasonable, and this should of course be discussed with our non-participator. The ultimate worker response will depend on a number of variables, which are beyond the scope of this publication, e.g. overall aims and objectives of sessions; personal and group boundaries; interactional skills of workers; group decision making/sharing processes, etc.

We would like to state that the idea of forcing anyone to participate in games is anathema to us .... games should be fun and demand voluntary participation. Some young people, however, will need to be encouraged in a variety of ways. This can be exceptionally difficult where a young person's past experiences have, for whatever reason, not included play as a life skill, or where particular kinds of play, e.g. physical/exuberant, have been discouraged.

Workers should find the various sections in the Youth Games Book helpful in designing sessions which will attract non-participators. There is obvious potential in our introductory half hour, for a worker to be equipped with a number of techniques which might facilitate this.

Puzzles and two-player games could be used for this purpose, e.g. Height of the 9×2p pieces, Triangles, One in the Middle, The Football Team. Visually interesting equipment like Water Games can also be used to encourage non-participators. Some will be quite happy to participate **on their own** by e.g. using a water game. Electronic Pin tables are renowned in youth social work circles for their potential as one player games which can keep group non-participators happily occupied without feeling excluded from the group gaming. Expensive pieces of equipment they might be, but a tremendous resource if you can get hold of one. Try Rebound as a poor substitute!

Gaming sequences can be used at various points in any particular session, e.g. at the beginning, middle, end, etc. Games can also be heavily used on special occasions like parties, visitor's nights, etc. A large group may well be split into sub-groups for activity sessions, discussion or relationship gaming. Such groups will often gather together at the end of an evening to play games and thus share an enjoyable experience.

3 puzzles and 2-player games

PUZZLES AND TWO PLAYER GAMES

The idea of being stuck in the mini bus with the chants of "…. why were you born at all…." rising in volume gives every adult who works with youngsters the occasional nightmare. And, as most of us know only too well, it **does** happen! The situation raises important questions regarding why we are not equipped with a few tactical interventions aimed at getting the folk in the bus to enjoy the next half an hour, or so, rather than having to loudly voice their boredom. But, then perhaps we do have the means to amuse and participate with kids in any situation where nothing much seems to be going on. In the section entitled: 'Group Games' we hope that a number of the games described will have fairly universal applications - remember, they don't always have to be used as formal class or group activities. Similarly, in this section we have tried to detail a range of activities which are often ideal boredom-breakers or time-fillers. When sensibly used, they will provide a valid shared experience and in many cases although the game may be relatively mundane, you may find yourself the originator of yet another 24-hour wonder!

In this section, the most elaborate equipment you will require for most of the games and puzzles is paper and pens, or a box of matchsticks, a pack of cards or a pocketful of loose change. We can almost guarantee that some of the fiendish little puzzles mentioned in the first part of the chapter will be tried by various species of youth workers on their unsuspecting bar-propping friends. Back in the youth group, we have discovered that an age-old basic love, which almost all kids share is a good 'trick'. Hopefully, the ones we offer will fit up a good many sleeves!

LATERAL THINKING

Originally, we believe that this name was coined by Edward De Bono for his own curious brand of side ways thinking. College common rooms were badly afflicted with the disease in the late nineteen-sixties as devilish situations were dreamed up by the problem setters. The idea is slightly derivative of 'What's my line', in that the group or individual can ask questions of the problem setter and they receive an answer, phrased as YES, NO or IRRELEVANT. The winner is the person who first successfully reaches the successful solution to the original statement. It sounds a bit odd, but it's an extremely easy technique to master and because most of the examples we have listed deal extensively with death and deception, they obviously have immediate appeal to simple, child-like minds!

For instance, the problem-setter might say:

"A man is lying dead in the middle of a road with a pack on his back. How did he die?"

Questions might follow this statement, as follows:

Q: Was he run over?
A: No
Q: Is the road relevant?
A: No
Q: Is the pack relevant to his death?
A: Yes
Q: Is it a ruck-sack?
A: No
Q: Was anyone else involved in killing the man?
A: No
Q: Did he commit suicide?
A: No
Q: He died accidentally?
A: Yes
Q: Was his pack too heavy for him?
A: No
Q: Did he fall from a height?
A: Yes
Q: Was it a parachute pack?
A: Yes
Q: And it failed to open?
A: That's right.

The problems are often based around the taken-for-granted way in which the questioners' interpret the information they are given. Once they start to enquire more searchingly about the basic original statement, a patch of light may be discovered at the end of the tunnel.

We have included a few problems and their solutions on the next pages. They are only examples and some require a different background of knowledge than others. The group solution finding process can be quite enlightening to the youth worker, especially when one realises that **younger** children veryfrequentlydo better at these lateral deductions than the adolescent age range. The time which it takes a group of 3 or 4 youngsters to find the answer they are seeking can vary considerably, but we normally allowed about ten minutes to quarter of an hour for the straight-forward problems and longer for the more convoluted specimens.

LATERAL THINKING PROBLEMS

1) Q: There is a body floating in a liquid. A man is annoyed because of this. Why?

   A: There's a fly in the man's soup.

2) Q: Two dwarves are in a large area, with sawdust on the ground and a plank is on the ground. One dwarf is smiling, the other is dead. Why did the dwarf die?

   A: The dwarf who is dead worked in a circus and he was worried about getting taller. Every day he measured himself against a plank which was exactly his height. The dwarf who is smiling wanted the circus job, so he sawed the plank through, so that it would appear that first dwarf had grown. The circus dwarf measured himself against the plank, thought that he was growing and committed suicide.

3) Q: A man with a towel around his waist is standing next to a horse. What is he doing?

   A: There are at least two possible answers. (1) He is letting his clothes dry out on a clothes horse, OR (2) he has just finished a gym session on the vaulting horse.

4) Q: There is a man hanging by a rope from the ceiling, with his feet two feet above the ground. He is dead. In the corner of the room, out of reach, is a bucket and in the middle of the room, underneath the feet of the man is a pool of water. How did he die?

   A: He froze a bucket of water, turned the bucket upside down, and let it slightly melt. He then put the bucket in

the corner of the room and stood on the melting ice
with the rope around his neck.

5) Q: Anthony and Cleopatra are lying on the floor. Around
them is broken glass and water. What has happened?

A: Anthony and Cleopatra are goldfish, their goldfish bowl
has been broken.

6) Q: Every day a man returns home to his flat, gets in the lift
and goes up to the 7th floor, gets out and walks up
another 3 floors to his flat.
Why?

A: He's a dwarf and he cannot reach higher than the 7th
button for the lift.

7) Q: Man goes into a bar and asks for a drink and the barman shoots off a gun into the air. The customer says "thanks".
Why?
A: He had hiccups and the bang made them go away!

8) Q: There is a man who goes to a Doctor's surgery and asks to have his arm amputated. Why?
A: Three men were shipwrecked in a small rowing boat with no food. One man was a surgeon and he was chosen as the person to amputate one arm from each person to use as food. When it came to his turn they had reached an island, but since they had agreed that **each** provide an arm, the surgeon had to have his arm cut off on his return to civilisation.

PUZZLES

Frustrating your neighbour, colleague or best friend is a pretty popular pastime. Doing this using the medium of paper and pencil, matchstick, coin and playing card puzzles etc. has a certain enjoyment value which can be devoid of spitefulness, since it is distinctly possible that the person who is on the receiving end the first time round will very soon be the protagonist.

On a slightly evil note, think how clever all your youngsters are going to think you are when you start plying them with these problems! More seriously, you may be pleasantly surprised how well these can work with introverted youngsters,who don't much like getting involved with the group, but who, nonetheless are highly delighted with the opportunity of pitting their wits against you at a quite intimate level.

MATCHBOX LIFT

This requires a little bit of practice, but once that has taken place it is quite addictive. The idea is to lift up one match box onto another one (which is on end) keeping the central finger firmly on the table at all times. The matchbox which is to be lifted must be gripped between the 2nd and 4th fingers.

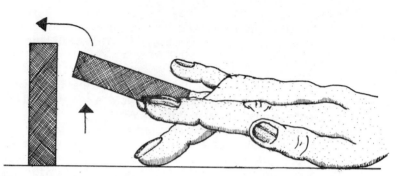

Three tips:

a) Keep the matchbox to be lifted close to the one which is going to serve as a pedestal.
b) Keep the pressure firmly on the central finger.
c) Angle the two fingers used for gripping so that the front of the matchbox is tilted upwards and therefore is more likely to make it to the top.

With even more practice you can do this with a matchbox and a king-size pack of cigarettes!

HEIGHT OF THE 9 2 PENCE PIECES

"You can con most of the people most of the time." In this case, it seems true. The puzzle is a 'one-off'. You must get everyone in a room, group, club, party or whatever to make a guess as to which coin when stood on its side, out of

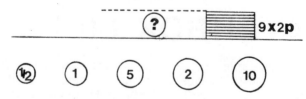

is exactly the same height as a pile of 9 two pence pieces.

We're going to ask you to try it
we bet 10p you're wrong!!

MATCHBOXES

This one is a brain teaser although once the answer is known it appears stupidly simple.

The aim is to place six match boxes in a combination so that each one touches every other one.

The solution we know is this:

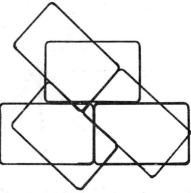

TRIANGLES

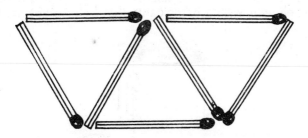

We're sure that you've been annoyed by this sort of puzzle before.

The aim is to move only **3** matches to make 3 absolutely new triangles.

The solution is rather in the order of the Lateral thinking problems. You can pick up any three matches and reach the answer as below. As you can see, you must be thinking 3-dimensionally.

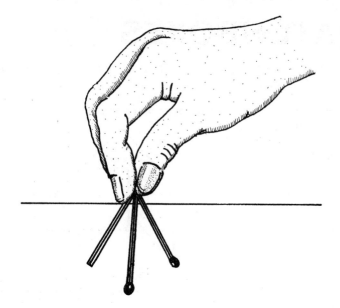

BALANCING COINS

The answer to this one makes use of a bridge-building principle, but don't tell your willing participants that before they start.

The aim is to place a pile of at least nine 2 pences on top of the £1 note at a central point (x in the diagram) across the top of the mug. The contestant may not hold the £1 note while trying to balance the coins, nor may other items be used to hold the £1 note in place.

To perform the amazing feat, the balancer must be provided with a fairly new £1 note. The solution requires corrugating the note to provide a sturdy platform for the coins:

THREE KNIVES

This is 'borrowed' from De Bono. Apologies. It's a great item if you can provide enough milk bottles, knives and glasses and don't have anyone in your group who knows the solution.

For each contestant or group you need 3 knives, three milk bottles and a glass - for safety and financial reasons, probably unbreakable. The aim is to balance the glass on the knives, which in turn are on the bottles. The tops of the bottles are just a little more than knife's distance apart and form a triangle.

The answer is cunning and involves an appreciation of weaving. Based on the same principle as closing up the flaps on a cardboard box, the knives are knitted together, so they provide a firm platform. In this shape they can be rested across the tops of the 3 bottles and easily support a carefully placed glass.

The knives are linked like this:

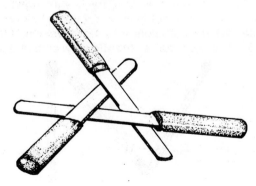

FOUR STRAIGHT LINES

The problem is to draw a continuous line, comprising of four straight line sections to connect every dot together. These straight lines may cross each other, but not double back i.e.

⋈ is O.K.;   ⋀⋉is incorrect

The answer is pure lateralism:

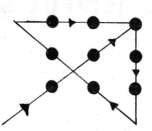

NUMBER 6

This can misfire if the kids you try it with don't have a basic knowledge of numbers, but in most groups it has resulted in a fair laugh for all. Ask the participants to move two out of the 3 matches to make 6. The wording is intentionally ambiguous. So is the answer:

THE STAR

A quickie! Snap 4 matches, but don't pull them apart. Gently bend the broken matches, so that the joint bends freely. Then place them on a smooth topped table (not mother's best) in the following shape:

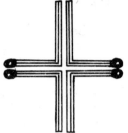

Tell your onlookers that they must rearrange these matches into a star shape WITHOUT touching them.

The answer is to pour a small quantity of liquid into the centre 'X' of the matches. To achieve the required result, the liquid must be very carefully applied at this intersection. Then, sit back and the matches will behave as an automaton. It may take a couple of minutes to work, so be patient.

BLACK MAGIC

Appealing to younger children, this is a cunning little oddity which requires two accomplices who are supposedly in telepathic contact with one another. What happens is that one of the team goes out of the room while the other stays with the audience, who are invited to choose an object for the outside telepath to recognise. Once the object has been chosen, the person outside the room returns and the 'telepath' who knows what the object is, starts asking their accomplice, "Is the object this...?". Each time the answer is "No", until there is a black coloured object mentioned. Then, the **next item** indicated will be the one which was agreed upon at the outset.

Everyone realises that they are being tricked, but how it is done can keep the group guessing for some time. The accomplice in the room, must, to maintain the secret vary the "black" objects around, otherwise the way in which the subterfuge has been perpetrated is rather obvious.

ELEVEN AND SIXTEEN

Mathematicians can feel free to write in and explain to us how this one works. Whatever the mechanics, it is a fine trick and comes courtesy of Colin, a part-time Lothian Youth leader.

To commence the action you say that you are going to randomly deal out the pack into piles across a table top. Make sure that you don't try to copy us too perfectly - we were left wondering why the trick wouldn't work for nearly quarter of an hour before realising that the pack was not numbering fifty-two! When you deal out the cards, face up, you in fact are making piles which add up to 11, based on the first card dealt. So, if you place down a 4 **you then add another 7 cards;** if it is as an Ace, **add 10 cards** with a Jack or King etc, you would add only **1** card.

Do this until the pack looks as though it is running out and then make a comment, such as: "That should be enough piles for you to choose from," at which point you separate the discards and leave them to one side.

Ask the 'client' to choose **3** piles and turn them over, while you have your eyes closed. Before the piles are turned over ask the person to look at the top card from each of the 3 piles and total up the score value which they have without telling you the score. The piles can be moved from their present position, it makes no difference. You then pick up all the cards in the other piles including discards and deal them out in piles across the table. Appear to be putting them in different size piles for some reason, while in fact you are counting up to 16. Once you reach 16, re-start the counting and the number of cards you are left with is the TOTAL SCORE count of the 3 cards in the 3 face down piles placed presently at the bottom of each pile.

DAVID LOVEL

This effort is brought to you by Christine Brotherston, an East Lothian youth club member - we thought that it was fascinating and unusual.

First Ask your victim to shuffle a pack of cards. Then deal out ten pairs of cards, face downwards.

Secondly Request that a card be taken from the top of two of the pairs. These should be memorised and then replaced as a **New Pair,** the remaining two cards also being replaced as a pair. (This process takes place while the magician, or whatever, turns away).

Thirdly All the cards are picked up and the pile is then dealt out following the memorised dealing system, as follows. The first card is placed at 'D' in **D**AVID; the second goes to the other 'D' position at the end of DAVI**D**. The third card is put at 'A' in 'D**A**VID' and the fourth goes to the other 'A' which is in **A**BBEY. This dealing sequence continues until all the cards have been placed into the 5 x 4 distribution. The last cards to be placed will be the two 'B's in A**BB**EY.

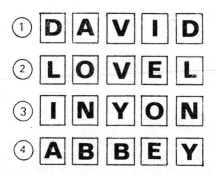

FinallyOnce all the cards are positioned, ask the assistant to state which row or rows their original pair of cards are now in. Armed with this information, as long as you can remember the mnemonic, you can immediately spot the two cards by finding the only two letters which appear either in the one or two rows indicated. It's so devious that the result is highly impressive and no-one will ever guess how the trick is done.

ONE IN THE MIDDLE

A well known card trick can still be one of the best. Taking a pile of cards which is a multiple of three, say 21, deal the cards into 3 piles face upwards and while this is being completed, ask a friend to memorise a card. At the end of the distribution, the 'client' indicates which pile, out of the 3, the chosen card is in. You then casually pick up the 3 piles, but be very careful that the chosen pack is placed in the **middle**. Repeat this process twice more, after which you deal out the cards from the pack (which is face down). Stop at the card which is the higher side of the midway point i.e. with 21 cards the hidden card is 11. When 'finding' the card at the end of the sequence it is best to appear to be scrutinising each card carefully, before finally making the selection.

YOU TOO CAN BE A MAGICIAN

Out of all our 'little tricks', this one had more appeal than we would have estimated. We had thought to exclude it from the collection, because if seemed a bit obvious, but its popularity made us decide otherwise.

You tell the 'client' that they have the ability to find cards in the pack. Fan out the whole pack, face downwards across a table top. Before doing this, have a careful look at the second or third card in from one end and memorise the value. Your first request to the new star performer is "Point to the......card." The value of this card is the one which you have already remembered. Pick up the card they point to but don't show it. Repeat this process, this time asking the person to point to whatever the value of the first card was. Pick up the card and ask for a third show of divination, asking for the value of the second card.

After this third effort, say "I'm going to find the......card" i.e. the value of the last card picked up. Fairly obviously, you now pick up the "plant" - the memorised card, near the end of the row. Look at the 4 cards in your hand and then show them to the amazed new Master Magician, as proof of their new powers!

ISLANDS

We were told about this one and managed to make a mistake in the rules first time around. But then Michael, the originator of the trick met us just before the manuscript had to go to the binders, and here we are again!

You have to tell the audience a little story. Take the 4 top value cards of each suit A, K, Q, & J and deal them into their respective suits, laid out so that the value of each card is showing. Once this is done, tell the audience that each suit represents a tribe who live on a different island. Up until now there has been no contact between the tribes. Then you put the 4 piles together one suit on top of the next and say that there has been a war and the tribes get rather mixed up! Shuffle the pile in the following manner; taking any number of cards from the top of the pile, place them besides the main pile, place the rest of the main pile on top of them. You can repeat these sequences as often as you like and invite the audience to join in. Say to them that something amazing has happened. All the islanders have decided to live in peace. Then deal out the cards into 4 piles, 1st card in each pile first, then 2nd etc. The result is a complete mix, 4 different suits/tribes, each with the same balance of Ace, King, Queen and Jack represented in each pile.

WHICH PICTURE CARD?

check the width of this margin

Budding graphic artists and students of antique games para-phernalia will no doubt have noticed that the printing on old playing cards and the like tends to be eccentric. A card trick can be based on the misalignment of printing on the court or Picture cards in an old pack. Its rather reminiscent of 'find the lady', but face upwards. Place three court cards in a row; it doesn't matter what values you use. With you not looking, challenge the audience to move any card round e.g. the Jack.

Obviously, with playing cards there is no difference between one end and another, or is there? When you, as the card-master, turn round, you carefully scrutinise the cards. What the audience do not realise is that there is a minute difference in margin width between one end of each card and the other, so on turning round the movement can be recognised. When originally setting out the cards, you must be careful to put all the cards around the same way, i.e. with the large or small width margin at the top.

COIN PUZZLES

There are a large number of these in existence, many of which are of the "in the fewest possible moves... variety." We do not intend to duplicate the books which cover this subject, but we include some examples so that you are aware of the style. Perhaps you could invent some of your own.

CHANGEOVER

With the following formation, move only 3 coins to reverse the triangle so it points down rather than up. It might even win you a coke!

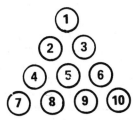

A)   Move 7 to the left of 2; 10 to the right of 3 and 1 to the bottom of 8 and 9.

Easy when you know how!

ROLL OVER

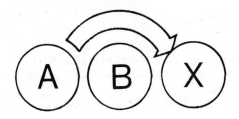

This is a 'once only' guessing game.

Place two coins A & B together and ask if the A coin is rolled around the B coin will it be upside down; upright or sidewise when it reaches the other side? To do it easily, try it on a carpet or similar.

A) Try it and find out!

COIN FOOTBALL

Ever since we gave up classroom darts games, using rather decrepit compasses and other more unmentionable pursuits, we thought that we had forgotten completely about coin football. A couple of recent journeys with the kids on the renowned "earth-shrinking 125" from Edinburgh to London have changed all that!

So, coin football. The rules are as varied as any other traditional game. The pitch is any smooth table top. Usually a number of large coins (say 3 x 2p's for each team) are used as players, heads for one team, tails for the other. Then, the ball is a ½ or 1p. The players may be propelled with a flick of the finger as in Subbuteo or with a short plastic or wooden ruler. The latter method, if rulers are available, makes the game fairer.

The duration of the game is decided and sides are chosen. 5 minutes each half is probably long enough. Players are positioned by hand before a kick off, then with no opposing players within 3" of the ball, the 'player' taking kick-off is shoved on to the ball which is kicked up the field.

One kick per turn is the rule, unless:-
1) the ball is kicked into another player on the same team.
2) a free kick has been awarded.

Fouls are given for:-

1) touching the ball with the ruler.
2) touching an opposition player with the ruler.
3) hitting an opposition player with a player **before** striking the ball.
4) moving a player by hand, except where allowed for in the rules.

At free kicks, any players may be re-positioned by hand, but opposition players must be at least 3" away from the ball.

Throw Ins become in this game, 'kick-ons'. This happens if the ball goes out of play over the side lines. Corner kicks and Goal kicks are taken as in real football and constitute an opportunity to reposition players and the 3" rule applies.

After a goal it is a kick off from the centre mark.

We found that as a journey-shrinker this game did us more good than British Rail!

KERCHECK

A 2 player game which we found popular with a mixture of I.T., YOP and Youth Club kids. Use a normal draught board and lay out 1p's and 2p's as indicated.

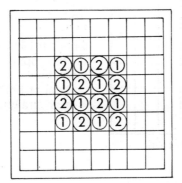

The rules are:

1) Coins can move one square, horizontally, vertically or diagonally.
2) Moving **away** from an opposing coin means that it is captured.
3) You may only move if you can move away from an opposing coin.
4) The game ends when neither player makes a capture.
5) The player with most pieces left wins.

Since the rules are a reversal of those used in most games it therefore adds to the interest value.

REVERSI

This is the two player game upon which the commercial 'Othello' mentioned elsewhere in this book is based. An 8 x 8 or 10 x 10 board can be used and the game is played using coins. 'Heads' and 'tails' determine ownership and the idea is to cover the board with more of your pieces. The Summer Scheme at Canongate was 'Proving Place' for this game and it was a successful alternative to its more expensive counterpart.

The idea is to make sandwiches. You can place a coin with either head or tail showing, anywhere where it will enclose any number of the opponent's coins. This placement may be diagonal, vertical or horizontal as long as it is in a straight line.

STARTING POSITION

You may only go if you can make a sandwich and when you do this you turn over all the coins between your two coins. It is quite possible to make more than one line at a time. It is equally and annoyingly likely that you will sometimes make sandwiches which will benefit your competitor more than you. If you **can** make a sandwich you must go. Play continues until all the spaces are filled.

See Othello (Commercial Games) for more comments.

SQUARE OF 5

With coins set out as below, rearrange them so that they are in a square where you can count 5 along each side.

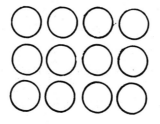

The answer is:

CHINESE REBELS

Very much in the fox and geese family of two player games this is useful as a simple diversion with all age groups. The board is simple to draw on a large piece of paper and 20 counters or coins of one sort are needed and one of a different type.

The general and the rebels all move one circle forwards, backwards or sideways, **but** the general can also 'kill' rebels by hopping over them, at which point they are removed from the board. No piece may move diagonally.

The general aims to either reach camp or to kill enough rebels to make himself safe. The rebels try to surround the general or corner him, so that he can't move.

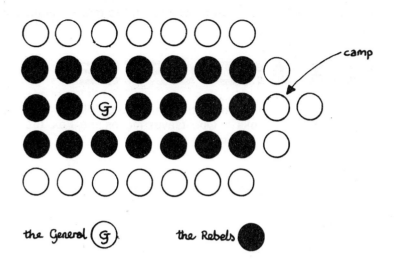

the General (G).   the Rebels ●

Not a bad game, though not one which is likely to become a regular favourite. Certainly it is a useful addition to the repertoire.

GOMUKU

This is large scale noughts and crosses. It is an alternative which is popular with younger groups. A photocopied board/sheet of paper is quite a good idea if your employer is feeling benevolent. Draw up a board with 19 horizontal lines.

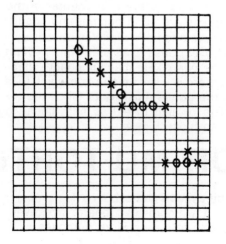

After this, place noughts and crosses on the intersection. 5 in a line wins.

FOX AND GEESE

One of the traditional games, this can also be played with coins, buttons or tiddly-winks . One player moves the Fox, the other moves the Geese. The board is:

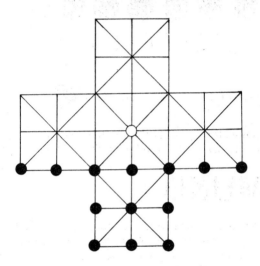

The fox is represented by the one counter in the centre of the board and the geese are 13 in number and positioned as above. All pieces may move one point along an unobstructed line. The fox must try to jump over geese to a vacant spot beyond, which knocks that goose off the board. He may jump more than one goose per turn, as long as there is a vacant point on which to land. The player who is moving the geese must try to block the fox in, so that he cannot move. The fox aims to 'eat' so many geese that there are no longer enough to block him in.

PIT OR MU-TORTURE

This is said to be a maori game, but as it is simple and two players can play it on any improvised board, whatever the size, it is thoroughly suitable for youth work purposes.

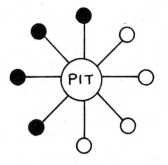

The aim is to make it impossible for your opponent to go. Start with 4 pieces each (of different colours) on adjacent points of the star shape. (only one piece at a time is allowed in the Pit)

A piece may be moved on to a next adjacent star point
OR
into the PIT, or out of the pit onto another star point. A piece can only be moved into the PIT when one or both of the adjacent star points are occupied by an opponent's piece.

Play ceases when one player cannot move. The game is more intricate and lasts longer than you might expect.

NINE MEN'S MORRIS

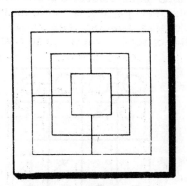

Draw up a board, as above, then with nine coins each (heads and tails), this game is easily improvised. Each player puts one coin in turn on an empty point (an intersection between two lines) on the board. The aim is to make a line of 3, at which point that player may remove an opponent's coin. (This should be a coin which is **not** in a line of 3 unless there is no other coin available). Once all the counters have been played, players move one of their pieces to a neighbouring point. They still try to make rows of 3 and rows can be broken and remade with the same diminishing effect on the opponent's force. Blocking an opponent so that they cannot move, or reducing the opponent to less than 3 coins ends the game.

ROMAN DRAUGHTS

They don't come much simpler than this! For 2 players. Jumping over opponent's pieces removes them from the board. As with draughts, reaching the backline allows players to move forwards or backwards. A move is one square or a hop. The aim is to remove all the opposing pieces, or to force a draw.

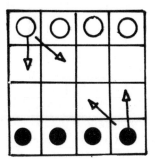

THE FOOTBALL TEAM

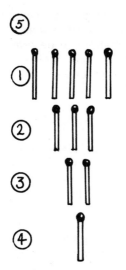

Matchsticks do look a little like men, and in the above formation they represent the old-fashioned 'line-up' of a football team. Ask your kids to re-arrange them moving only 4 matches, so that the entire team is facing in the opposite direction. The answer Involves moving a single match in ROW 4 to ROW 5 and then 3 matches move from ROW 1 to ROW 3 and that's it.

NIM

The same formation can be used for a two player game. Choose who goes first, then that player may remove any number of matches from a line, including the whole line. The other player does the same and the aim is **to leave the opponent with the last match.** The game is quite annoying, but popular with a wide age range, since it is so easy to play even if making sure you win is more of a problem.

KAYLES

Another matchstick game for two. Between 20 and 30 matches are normally used. The matches are placed in a long row end to end and on each turn one match can be removed, or two if they are touching. That's the only rules. Unlike in the game of NIM, the winner is the person who picks up the last match.

MAXEY

This is a good game. There, we have committed ourselves!! 7 parallel lines should be drawn on a piece of paper, each should be roughly the length of a match and they should be slightly less than a match-length apart. Each player has 5 matches and the paper should be placed so that the lines point towards each player. One match is played at a time and they are placed along the lines with the match heads pointing towards the player. If two matches are side by side, then a player may opt to play a match resting across the two. This is done with the match head pointing to the right.

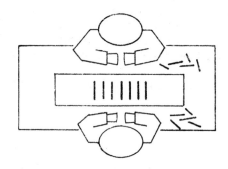

Scoring is as follows: 1 point for each match played adjacent to another match. 2 points for each match played across adjacent matches.

The highest scoring player is the winner.

GALE

David Gale, associate Professor in Maths at Brown University in the States invented this little diversion. It is a game of strategy and involves 2 players using different coloured pens or pencils. In the diagram above, the solid dots represent those belonging to Player A and the small circle dots are those for Player B. The direction of play for each player is also shown on the diagram. Taking alternate turns, each player joins any 2 of his or her dots together with a single line. This can only be done in either a horizontal or vertical direction. Whilst Player A is trying to join the bottom and top sides of the grid together, Player B is trying to join up the left and right sides.

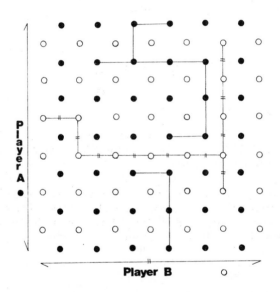

The winner is the first player to make a continuous line joining their 2 sides together. No lines may cross.

This is an ideal alternative game to the well known 'boxes' syndrome. With "Sprouts" described elsewhere in this book, they form   quick paper and pencil games which will be new to most young people.

SPROUTS

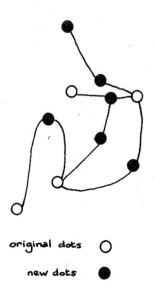

original dots   O

new dots   ●

Originating from Cambridge, this has proved a successful paper and pencil game in almost all settings with a wide range of age groups.

To start with about 5 or 6 dots are drawn on a piece of paper. Taking alternate turns, 2 players draw a line either joining two dots or joining a dot to itself. They then draw a new dot in anywhere along the line they have just made.

There are 3 rules:

1) No line may cross itself, or cross a line that has already been made.
2) No line may be drawn through a dot.
3) A dot may only have 3 lines leaving it.

The last person who can successfully draw a legitimate line is the winner. The game is more fun than 'boxes' and nowhere near as widely known.

CROSSWORDS

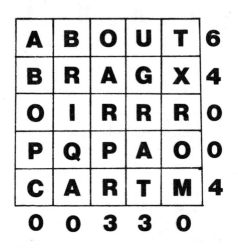

A	B	O	U	T	6
B	R	A	G	X	4
O	I	R	R	R	0
P	Q	P	A	O	0
C	A	R	T	M	4

0   0   3   3   0

This is a painless form of word game which can be played by two players or more. Each player needs to draw a square 5 x 5 and then the paper is kept hidden. Each player in turn calls out a letter and everyone, including that player must write that letter in a square. Play continues until all the boxes are filled. The aim is to make words either horizontally or vertically. The shortest word which counts is 2 letters in length, the longest, obviously 5 letters. Each letter scores 1 point for a player when it is part of a word. A five letter word scores 5 plus 1 bonus. You may score more than one word in a line but they must not be touching; so it would have to be two, two-letter words with another letter in between.

GUGGENHEIM

As a contestant for the game with the most unbelievable title, this probably wins. But, since we believe it to be a classic time-filling group game, it is included. The bored, over-coffee session in the office or train trip can (we have experienced) provide a perfect setting for this game. As leader, you write down a key, five or six letter word across a page, for instance:-

then write 5 headings along the left of the page, e.g.

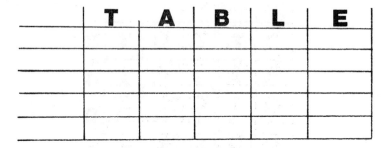

	T	A	B	L	E

All copy down the headings and in a set period of time each heading must have an entry beginning with the letter of the alphabet indicated by the 'Key word'. All acceptable words score, except where more than one person has submitted the same word, then neither person scores. The subtlety is to look for unusual words for your submissions.

MORA   SCISSORS, PAPER, STONE

Kids around the world will teach these games to adults if they are interested. It is surprising how quickly we unlearn our heritage.

Mora is a game of fingers. Players hold a closed fist against their chests, while facing one another. At a given signal they "throw" a number of fingers; a closed fist indicates 'O'. Simultaneously, they both shout a total for the two players' "throws." A cry of 'Mora" indicates ten. Fifteen rounds, or so, will give a clear winner and a slice of noisy fun.

We found that playing this with kids gave rise to disputes, but even with us acting as referees didn't wholly avoid the problem. Let us know if you find the answer. (The game can be played calling odds or evens and one or two hands can be used. Obviously a draw is very likely in this variation).

Scissors, paper, stone can start the same way as Mora, or the hands can be held behind the back. At the signal, both players display their hand either as a clenched fist (stone); a V (scissors) or as an open palm (paper). The pecking order for the hands is as follows:

PAPER ENCLOSES STONE
STONE BLUNTS SCISSORS
SCISSORS CUT PAPER
TWO SYMBOLS THE SAME IS A DRAW

Again a predetermined number of rounds is a good idea.

SPOOF

Like so many other games which we have enjoyed playing with kids this one started life in pubs (we think). There's nothing much simpler, yet it is a game which is not as commonly known as we expected.

Here goes.... Ask everyone (2 to 6 players) to take out 3 coins and explain to them that they must each place between 0 and 3 coins in a closed fist and place it on the table in front of them. This process is completed out of sight of the other players. Once all the players have put their mits on the table they each have a guess at the TOTAL NUMBER OF COINS in **all** the hands. No two people may choose the same number.

If someone guesses the correct number, they drop out and play continues with new arrangements of coins being made. If no-one makes a correct guess, everyone re-selects a new handful of coins or sweet nothingness. The person having first "guess" circulates around the group.

The final loser is the person left 'in', who has not found the correct number at any point during the game. With 2 players, it is best to play a best of 3 sequence. The loser in a pub will normally buy a pint; we played the game with kids' groups using forfeits. Six foot three adults crawling around the floor on their knees in a public coffee-bar muttering "Why was I born so small?" to the customers, seemed to amuse our teenagers. We can't understand why!

SNIPES

Snipes was first introduced to us by Mono and Scranner of the Canongate Youth Project. Definitely a game for hardmen (and women!) Snipes contains a strong sadistic element, so beloved of Scottish Youth!

Do not attempt to involve any more than six or seven people in the sequence - the reason for this will become apparent later. The game involves an element of chance and forfeit - playing cards are used to determine who gets "sniped" in each round.

If six people are playing, you will need six cards numbered say 2 - 7. One card is dealt face down to each player; they are then turned over. Number 2 card is the loser, and its recipient must suffer the forfeit. This involves each person in the group in turn taking the bundle of six playing cards and hitting the loser on the nose with them.

The rules governing "hits" are as follows:-
1. The playing cards must be held vertically, and should not be bent or "tensioned" in any way.
2. Only one attempt can be made by each person (unless the loser moves to avoid a hit, in which case, another turn is given).
3. Only the nose should be hit - if any other part of the face is touched by the cards then the loser takes a hit at the person who has broken the rules.

It is usual to play several rounds of Snipes - we have not heard of any injuries resulting from its use, but we would like to exonerate ourselves from any possible claims for damage! You have been warned!

KNUCKLY

Most people should remember this two player game. It involves players taking turns at rapping each other's knuckles with their clenched fist. Play commences with the players facing each other, either standing or seated. The fore arm should be outstretched with fist clenched and the back of the hand uppermost. The two players then move their fists together until the top joints of the fingers are touching.

One person is nominated to start, and tries to rap the other person's knuckles before they can be withdrawn. If he succeeds he continues to get another shot until he misses, at which point play passes to his opponent, and so on. An enjoyable but sometimes painful way of spending 10 minutes.

For those less masochistic however, an alternative method is to use open palms instead of clenched fists i.e., players move their finger **tips** together as opposed to joints and hence they would receive a slap from an open palm, much kinder than a rap from a clenched fist!

PITCH AND TOSS

One of the very regional games much associated with either being young or gambling, depending upon from where you have come.

It's an alternative, or derivation of the simple heads or tails coin-toss. In the form we give below it is also reputed to be a Scottish pastime, though it probably evolved during the first World War. Once taught to kids it can spread back into the classroom world, so you may be given reason to look furtive when the new source of debate reaches the staffroom or the P.T.A. meeting!

A piece of wood is stuck in the ground, or a bottle is laid on the floor about 10 yards away. Coins are thrown (pitched) and the person who has thrown the nearest coin to the target is allowed to pick up all the coins, place them along the forearm and then toss them from this place into the air. All the coins landing on the ground as heads are then traditionally regarded as the pitch and tosser's property. Those left over were used for another toss, by the 2nd closest pitcher until all are accounted for.

LEG WRESTLING

This competitive 2 player sequence is a test of strength and operates well as a spectator event.

Two volunteers are required to lie on the floor, side by side, in the centre of the circle. They should be lying in opposite directions to each other player. The two legs are then crooked round each other at the back of the knee joint, and battle commences!

The aim is simply to exert sufficient leg pressure sideways to throw your opponent off balance and force his leg over onto the ground. There is a marked similarity to arm wrestling - but it's much more fun with legs.

MOTOR CAR/ MINI-BUS GAMES

DRIVING BLIND

The driver silently chooses an object in the distance and tells all the passengers to close their eyes (not the driver's, NOTE!). Each passenger can then open their eyes whenever they like and call out "NOW". The player who is nearest in distance and time to the driver's object is the winner and scores a point. A complete game can be up to any number of points as agreed beforehand.

GUESS THE DISTANCE

We hadn't thought of this one, but it's quite an obvious game for journeys. An object in the distance is chosen and each occupant guesses the distance from a given moment in time. The most accurate guess, based on the milometer reading is the winner. We hope that your local authority bus has a dial that works!

PUB SIGNS

This is based on having good eyesight and some imagination. All the occupants of the vehicle look out for pubs and win a point if they are the first to correctly name the pub. Signs are often misleading, so it often takes 3 or 4 guesses from different passengers to get it right. Score one point per correct sign. Any advance on the "Shoulder of Mutton and Cucumber"?

SUMS

Passengers take turns to 'adopt' a car registration number as it is passed by or passes the car or mini-bus. Say for instance John's car has a registration XYZ 249, he scores 2+4+9=15. The aim of the game is to be the first player to obtain an EXACT score of **50**; 51, or 52 etc won't count and going over takes a player back to zero. An endless sort of affair, it can be played anywhere there are other vehicles, which gives it an advantage over 'Pub Signs' in the more remote county regions.

A second version can be played if you have paper and pencils for each player. Again each player adopts a number plate of successive passing cars, but this time the number element is written down as a number with units, tens and hundreds i.e. GMK 192 becomes 192. On the next car or van, or whatever that the player adopts, 192 is added to the new number, say 940; i.e.

```
  192
+940
─────
 1132
─────
```

This process is continued up to a limit. We suggest 50,000, which if it works, keeps a whole mini-bus occupied throughout a trip. The first contestant with a score over 50,000 wins.

4 the 'heavy end'

THE HEAVY END

(see note on page 10 and the
Relationship Games Introduction
pp 13-16 before using games from
this section).

MAGIC SHOP

Much of the success of this small group role play depends on the leader's ability to encourage others to identify their individual strengths and weaknesses. Although this process should be an honest one, difficulties may arise where, e.g. a group member is prone to being scapegoated by others. These issues must be considered prior to using "Magic Shop", and the maturity of the group gauged. If in doubt, don't use it - there's always another games session!

The gaming element in this role play involves individuals trading for personal quality with a "shopkeeper", who should be nominated by the leader. The shopkeeper trades individually with each person in the group and should therefore be a competent actor, capable of varying the responses to each person and of "putting on a good show". For these reasons the leader may initially wish to nominate an adult who can act as a model for future shopkeepers.

Start the ball rolling by explaining the purpose of the Magic Shop - to swap a bit of a personal quality you've got a lot of for a bit of something you're lacking. So someone with an awful lot of energy might swop for some patience. At this point the group could discuss each individual's strengths and weaknesses, before nominating the first person to trade with the shopkeeper. Alternatively, the trading can start right away, with just a few minutes being spent with each person helping them work out what they want to swop.

Role Plays can often be made easier for adolescents if there are one or two props around - e.g. a table for the shopkeeper to use as his counter; and because role play is so unstructured, it's a good idea for the leader to direct operations - they will have a much better idea than anyone else of what is required to make the Magic Shop a realistic scenario. Little things can be important, like asking each player to leave the room and make an entrance into the Magic Shop.

After the initial session, there is scope for discussing people's awareness of personal qualities in themselves and in others. For those who are keen to develop the role play with the group, you could try creating two or three person scenarios with players acting out their newly gained qualities.

Average time: half an hour minimum.

GROUP MIME GAME

This works well as a spectator event with a large group, but it can easily be used with smaller ones. Mime cards need to be prepared in advance and these can be designed to cater for the group's interests, allowing the Mime Game to be used with diverse groups and ages.

Some examples of Mime cards are as follows:-

2 People: A shopkeeper refusing to sell you cigarettes in his shop.
Two wrestlers
Saying goodnight to your girl/boy friend.
Having a talk with your social worker.

3 People: 2 policemen arresting someone in the street.
A Mr Universe contest
Playing Frisbee
Getting served in a fish and chip shop

4 People: Escape from prison - 2 prisoners, 1 warden, 1 dog
A team of acrobats
Closing time in a pub - 1 barman, 3 customers
A children's hearing (juvenile court)

5 People: A pop group
Your own group
People at a football match
Making a film - 1 director, 1 cameraman, 3 actors

Players should be numbered off e.g. 1-15, and corresponding cards are put in an envelope. The person introducing the game picks out a mime card at random and then takes out as many numbers from the envelope as are necessary to do the mime. People whose number comes up must leave the room to rehearse their mime. On their return, the mime is performed in front of the group - it can be treated purely and simply as a spectator exercise, or the group can be asked to guess what the mime is.

This type of sequence is very popular, and always produces a few laughs. On the growth side, it is excellent for encouraging self confidence and co-operative activity skills.

Allow half an hour or so.

SITUATIONS

A useful discussion technique which encourages the group to look at particular social situations, and how effectively individuals cope with them. Suitable for small groups only, the "situations" are prepared in advance, and written out on cards. 20 cards should suffice for a small group.

Examples of thought-provoking situations are:-
"What would you do if your teacher accuses you of stealing something from the classroom. It wasn't you but you know who it was."
"What would you do if you find out that a friend of yours has been experimenting with drugs?"
"What would you do if a friend comes to you and says he has committed a serious assault and wants you to hide him from the police?"

Players should select a card in turn round the group. Each person can be asked to state how they would handle the situation - and this can be discussed by the whole group. Alternatively, each person can be asked to   act out their situation with another member of the group. In either case, it can be useful to tape record the discussion and play it back towards the end of the session so that e.g. any common theme can be picked up and elaborated.

A good sequence for increasing self-confidence and self expression. Situations can help establish group norms and provide increased awareness of "difficult" adolescent experiences. Allow at least half an hour.

COMPUTER

This is the classic relationship game for young people. If offers emotional stimulation and feedback, helps people communicate honestly with each other, and is adaptable to the chronological age, the size and the maturity of the group. It is also tremendous fun to play!

Adults must be prepared to spend time preparing computer cards for the sequence - and these can be easily designed to suit the particular characteristics of most groups, e.g. at various stages of development, introductory, established and advanced.

Some examples of cards are:-

INTRODUCTORY	ESTABLISHED	ADVANCED
The person with the knobbliest knees	The person you'd most like to have as your friend	The most honest person
The cuddliest person	The person who thinks they're a hard man, but aren't really	The person you've liked most this evening
The person with the nicest smile.	The biggest scrounger.	The person who finds it hardest to tell the truth.
The person you'd most like to be locked in a dark room with.	The person who usually gets a raw deal.	The person who always gets it wrong!

The sequence commences with the person introducing the game asking for a volunteer to select a card. The card is **not read aloud,** but should be handed on by the volunteer to the person that it "fits" best. So if the volunteer (in an established group) selects a card with "the person who's annoyed you most this evening" on it, he might well give it to Alan - because he's been hassling him all evening. Alan must then read the card out loud to the group, return it to the pile and take his turn at selecting the next card.

Players should be constantly encouraged to give their cards to the most appropriate person - and should be given feedback by the group as to the suitability of their choice. Some kids may need adult help to make the most appropriate choice, and this should be offered freely, until everyone is comfortable with the sequence.

Provided that you start a group off with introductory sequences, kids will rapidly get used to Computer, and will be prepared to debate, and ultimately accept as relevant, other people's perceptions of them. Moreover, this will take place in an atmosphere of mutual trust and enjoyment.

Computer is a relationship tool that can be constantly adapted as the group matures. It is worth spending a fair amount of time preparing the cards and designing them around your particular group's interests and attributes. Cards should ideally be hand-printed so that they can be easily read, and help should be given discreetly to anyone who has difficulty reading the cards. Adults should also be on the look-out for those who, towards the end of the sequence, have not yet received cards, does this mean that there has not been a suitable card for them, or have they been ignored for some other reason?

In an introductory version of Computer the games leader would probably want to use any trick in the book to make sure that each player is offered a card, even if it's a nasty one! The same leader in an advanced group might want to ask them why Paddy hasn't had a card and all Mary's have been a bit brutal!

Computer is infinitely capable of adaption - so much so that kids will often get into making their own sets of cards for parties or special group events.

The sequence, in an advanced group can be played with each person retaining the cards that have been given to them (instead of returning them to the pile). This enables the leader to invite people in turn, to read out the cards they have received and so encourage discussion and debate.

In interactional terms, the amount of material produced in an average computer session is immense, but it does take skill and the recognition and use of group dynamics, to enable young people to process this material productively. Computer, of course, should (like any other game) only be used in this way if it "fits in"

98

with the rest of the session, and the group's purpose.

It's possible for Computer to be played without cards in some advanced groups. This requires a volunteer to think of the first Computer phrase, which is then whispered to the first player who must say it out loud to the most appropriate person in the group. The receiver of the Computer phrase thinks of one to whisper to the next player, and so the sequence continues until everyone in the group has received at least one phrase.

Playing time in "standard" versions is dependant on the number of cards prepared and the size of the group. Try to allow 2 or 3 cards for each person.

FEAR IN THE HAT

This is a useful game for small group work and can easily be adapted to cover a range of emotions, e.g. "Love in a Hat", "Anger in a Hat", etc.

This sequence should only be attempted when you feel that the group are at the stage where they will be prepared to share some of their emotions with each other.

A game like this is a relatively easy way of introducing the idea of sharing emotions with friends and peers as an alternative way to acting out or repressing strong emotional feelings.

The sequence will need some kind of introduction by an adult, which should ideally be related to some activity or discussion where the group can be asked to identify what triggers off a particular emotion during a discussion or activity.

A pencil and a piece of paper are required for each person in the group, and the sequence commences with the leader asking the group to complete a sentence like "In this group I am afraid that......" (or in the case of "Anger in a hat", "in this group I get angry when......"). When everyone has completed their sentence, all the slips of paper should be put in a hat or similar receptacle. The receptacle is then passed round the group to each person, in turn, who selects a slip of paper reads out and then elaborates on it trying to express exactly what the person who wrote it was feeling. So after reading out a slip of paper which says e.g. "I am afraid that people slag (Criticise) me", someone might say "There's a lot of slagging in this group and that puts people off saying anything serious". If the group find this kind of individual feedback too threatening, the leader can stimulate a group discussion on the various factors that have been identified as triggering off anger, fear, etc.

The usefulness of this type of sequence arises from the material that is produced during play. Role play can easily be used instead of discussion, and leaders might like to give some feedback on the dynamics of the group, relating this also to emotional responses. It must be remembered that this style of groupwork necessitates adults sharing their own emotional responses with young people in the group.

Allow up to one hour.

CHINESE ROULETTE

An hour is needed for this guessing game. Because it involves describing characteristics of other group members, we would always classify it as a sequence for well-established groups. The game was used in an epic of the modern german cinema to illustrate the lack of communication and understanding within a group.

To start, one member of a group (there should be at least 5 in number for a good game) volunteers to answer questions as though they were another member of the group. The volunteer does not indicate who they are trying to be, and each group member in turn, asks one question which the volunteer tries to truthfully answer in the style of the chosen person. The game can be played with either one or two rounds of questions being asked, followed by a round of guesses, where each group member says who they think has been portrayed. They can, of course, say that it is themselves!

The style of the questions is important to the game and the best type of question starts: "If you were a colour, what would you be?" or "If you were going to commit suicide, how would you do it?" or "What sort of flower would you be?"

It's an interesting and varied game and it makes considerable demands on the actor, who is answering the questions. They must try really hard to get "inside" their chosen person, since the questions will relate to matters not normally considered. Making sure that everyone has been chosen as the subject is impossible, but at least the whole group should have felt involved since the sequence has a high 'games' level. Obviously, it should be played by a group who know one another fairly well. Was it Alan or Howie who was the Venus- Flytrap?

PERSONAL STATEMENTS

'Personal statements' is an excellent device for providing feedback, both positive and negative, to individual members of a small or large group. It is used most constructively by groups at an advanced stage of development, although the game can be used with groups who have not yet reached this stage by insisting that, e.g. only positive statements are made.

The person introducing the game should explain that one person is required to leave the group and go out of earshot. The remaining members of the group then suggest various statements which could be made about the person outside the group. The three most appropriate (or humourous! - with a less advanced group) are written down or committed to memory by e.g. the group leader. The person outside is then invited to come back into the group and listen to the three statements which have been made about her. She must then try to guess who made each of the statements. When this sequence has been completed the leader should nominate someone else to leave the group, and the sequence can continue until each person has had a chance to have statements made about them.

If the game is being played competitively, then the winner is the person who has the most correct guesses. (Allow 3 guesses at the author of each statement).

Workers attitudes and responses are important with this game to make sure that the game is used in a positive way. The usual practice is to suggest to the group that they make a couple of positive statements about each person and one critical (but honest) one. There are obvious opportunities for using personal statements in a small group as a personality feedback exercise, although this should only be done where the group leader is convinced that players are mature enough to handle this kind of issue.

Allow 30 minutes playing time minimum.

TRUTH, DARE, DOUBLE DARE, PROMISE, REPEAT, KISS, COMMAND

Most people will have played this game at some point in their lives, and should therefore be familiar with its concept. The sequence contains some of the challenging aspects of games like "The Truth Game" and "Computer", but there is a freedom of choice present which enables individuals to participate at different levels. The "difficult" categories for adolescents are likely to be: "Truth"; "Double Dare"; "Kiss"; and "Command".

Seven sets of cards are required - the sequence can be played with less, but this does restrict the range of choice. Some examples of suitable cards are as follows:-

TRUTH: The question on the card must be answered truthfully.

Is it true that you are lonely sometimes?
Is it true that you are shy with girls/boys?
Is it true that your best friend sometimes lets you down?

DARE: You must do what the card says.

I dare you to take off two articles of clothing.
I dare you to pretend you are having a shower.
I dare you to pretend you are a dog.

DOUBLE DARE: The person in charge of the cards must also do what the card says.

I double dare you to roll your trousers up to the knee for the rest of the game.
I double dare you to crawl on your hands and knees right round the room.
I double dare you to pick a partner and do a wee dance.

I DARE YOU
To PRETEND
YOU ARE
HAVING A
SHOWER.

PROMISE: Often applies to the future.

Promise to kiss someone goodbye when you leave the group tonight.
Promise to sing a song once the game is finished.
Promise to hold hands with someone till the game ends.

REPEAT: The words on the card must be repeated as fast as possible.

Repeat 3 times:
"The Leith police dismisseth us."

Repeat 3 times:
"I'm not a pheasant plucker, I'm a pheasant plucker's son, and I'm only plucking pheasants till the pheasant plucker comes".

Repeat 3 times:
"If Peter Piper picked a peck of pickled pepper, where's the peck of pickled pepper Peter Piper picked".

KISS: You must carry out the action specified on the card.

Give the person sitting on your right a peck on the cheek.
Ask the nearest person of the opposite sex to give you a kiss.
Pretend you are kissing the person of your dreams in the back row of the pictures.

COMMAND: More difficult than a dare, and the action **must** be carried out.

I command you to stand back to back with some friendly person and give each other a cuddle.
I command you to go up to someone you fancy and ask them to give you a big cuddle.
I command you to sit on the floor for the rest of the game.

Try to make up at least six cards in each of the seven categories - this will be more than enough for most small groups, and just about adequate for a large one. Like computer cards, these can be made more difficult and challenging to suit the ongoing development of the group - but don't forget the "funnies", as this keeps the interest level high.

One person in the group must take charge of the cards - remember that if anyone selects a Double Dare card, then the person in charge of the cards must perform the action as well. Initially, it is best if the cards are held by an adult.

The sequence commences with someone selecting one card from any of the seven bundles and following the instruction on the card. Thereafter, people should take a card in turn round the group. Players should be encouraged to carry out the action and not "pass", although it can be an idea to let the group know which are the easier categories.

"Truth, Dare, Double Dare, Promise, Repeat, Kiss, Command" should only be used with an established group. You will probably find that the group themselves will eventually be quite strict about not allowing people to "pass", and might even want to institute a system of penalties. This is O.K. as long as execution, and assault and battery is discouraged!

THE TELEPHONE GAME

This is another spectator type game which is best used with an advanced group. If kids are into playing this particular game, the results can be absolutely hilarious.

Much beloved of Panmure House, the Telephone game is usually played at the end of a session with a large group. It is eminently suitable for those youngsters born to showmanship who can rarely find a constructive outlet for their talent!

As a spectator exercise, it can work with as few as three or four people completing the sequence. As the game is used progressively during the life of a group, it will be found that other youngsters and adults can build up the appropriate skills required to make an utter and complete idiot of themselves in front of the rest of the group!

Ideally, the game should be played with the group sitting in a semi-circle with one empty chair in the centre. A volunteer is required to choose a card which has on it something like "I am a sex maniac" or "Is that why you phoned me at this time of night?", "I love you", "You really piss me off" etc.

The volunteer must then sit on the seat in the middle facing the group and pretend to be talking on the telephone to anyone of their choosing. However, they must end their conversation with the phrase on the card - and must try to have an imaginary conversation which makes some kind of sense. The sequence can be repeated as many times as there are volunteers.

An essential part of any spectator sequence, is that the group should be helped to provide encouragement for the person in the middle - who is, after all, providing free entertainment for everyone else. Adults can help in this process, and might like to show off their own acting talents in the sequence to provide a model for young people to copy and adapt.

SURVIVORS

Survivors is a small group role play technique which usually produces lively discussion. It places the group in the rather nasty situation where one person has to be sacrificed so that the rest can survive. The group task is to choose the most expendable person, and this is usually done by discussion which is centred on the various roles which have been ascribed to group members.

As with any role play, you should set the scene carefully and encourage the group to think themselves into the situation. Explain that the group are survivors of a holocaust - a hurricane or a nuclear explosion - and this has brought them together for the first time. A hurricane will have led to them being adrift at sea on a raft which will only continue to float if one person jumps overboard to certain death in the shark-infested waters! In the aftermath of a nuclear explosion, the group will have gathered together in a nuclear shelter where they will have to stay for a month until radiation levels are low enough to leave .... unfortunately, one person must leave the shelter immediately so that the air and rations will last out for the month.

Cards can be used to ascribe roles to players, e.g. farmer, doctor, labourer, social worker, plumber, scientist, etc. Tell the group that they must decide which person to sacrifice on the basis of the importance of each person's contribution to the new society. The leader should stress that drawing lots or volunteering is not allowed. Adults in the group should participate fully in the role play, and can provide a useful lead to others by adding depth to their particular character, e.g. a self-important scientist, an outraged businessman, etc.

'Survivors' can be an experience in itself, but has obvious potential as a lead-in to group discussions on societal roles, group decision making, etc. Due to its relatively unstructured nature, Survivors should only be introduced when the group feels secure with role play techniques.

Allow 20 minutes to half an hour minimum, after the introduction.

STORYTELLING

Verbal confidence can be built up using this sequence. Ideal for small groups, or as a spectator experience with 7 or 8 people from a large group. The aim of the game is to improvise a story, with each person telling a bit of it. The person introducing the game might want to start the story herself or nominate an adult to begin, so that players have an idea of what is expected from them.

The person starting the sequence should begin to tell a story, and should stop whenever he likes; the person on his right must then continue the story for a bit before stopping and handing over to the person on his right, and so on around the group until the story is finished.

If necessary, the leader can suggest a theme for the story, to make things easier e.g. a robbery, a love story etc. The material produced in story telling can be used for an improvised drama session, or can be tape recorded and played back to the group for their amusement. The leader might also want to initiate some kind of feedback session on individual's performances, as the story teller's expertise and confidence can be further built up in this way. The sequence itself can be repeated as required.

Allow 20 minutes or so for each story.

THE SILENCE GAME

Very much a small group experience for advanced groups of older adolescents, the Silence Game is a useful tool for stimulating discussion on non-verbal communication, group norms, personal limits. etc.

The aim of the game, simply put, is for the group to maintain absolute silence for as long as possible. The gaming element involves each group member writing down on a piece of paper the name of the person they think will be first to break the silence. Each player's own name should be written in a corner of the paper to enable discussion on e.g. who chose whom and why. This discussion can be initiated as soon as the silence is broken.

Care should be taken to ensure that the group will be left alone and without interruption for the duration of the game. The sequence is particularly useful for eliciting comment on what it feels like to be a member of the group in the absence of any verbal interaction. Discussion can be stimulated by questions like: "Did you feel uncomfortable with the silence?" "What were you thinking about?", "Did your thought stay in the room, or were you thinking about things outside the room?"

Just in case you happen to get lumbered with an exceptionally determined group of young people, it is best to state a maximum time limit for the silence exercise - 20 minutes is probably a realistic maximum.

BRAINSTORMING

These are not games as such but have been included in this section because they are basic groupwork techniques which can be used to produce a multitude of material for group discussion.

Brainstorming has the effect of encouraging group cohesion, by valuing each member's contribution equally. It creates a collaborative atmosphere rather than a competitive one.

A blackboard and chalk, and/or a large piece of paper and felt pen is necessary. The group can practice brainstorming by trying to imagine as many uses as possible for, e.g. a coke bottle, a shoe etc. The leader writes down the ideas as they are called out, omitting none. He throws in his own ideas and therefore remains a contributing member of the group. Two or three minutes should be allowed for the brainstorming sequence, after which the group can discuss the ideas produced, perhaps with a view to identifying the most practical ones.

With a large group, brainstorming can be played as a team game, each team having a leader. At the end of the session, the total for each team is announced. Teams can then be asked to decide in groups on their 5 or 10 most original ideas, and awarded points for ones not thought of by the other team.

Brainstorming can be used to help solve problems facing the group, e.g. "Where should we go for our camping weekend?" "What can we do to make the group more exciting?" etc. The technique can also be used to introduce the group to broad concepts by asking e.g. "If you were given £50,000 to spend on a new facility for the community, what would you spend it on?" Brainstorming can be used with any size of group at all stages of development.

QUESTIONNAIRES

These are a useful tool in initiating discussion on personal and relationship issues. Suitable only for small groups where initial trust has been established, care should be taken to guard against difficulties arising from any group members who lack proficiency in reading or writing. Questionnaires must be prepared in advance and should be as simple as possible with participants being asked e.g. to fill in a missing word, or tick the appropriate box. Adults in the group should participate fully and honestly in filling in their own Questionnaires.

Discussion can be initiated by exchanging questionnaires with the person on your right or left, and asking for both individual and group comment on particular responses.

Try Questionnaires like:-

I am ....
I think ....
I want ....
I feel .... ´
I need ....
etc

I am ...... at home
I am ...... at school
I am ...... in the group
I am ...... with my friends
etc

HUMAN SACRIFICE!

This is one of the 'we-wanted-you-to-stumble-across-it-by-mistake', variety of games. In fact it's not a game at all, rather it is Michael Bentine of Goons and "It's a Square World"fame's attempt to INVENT a game. If you explain the idea it can be a good fun exercise to play with your group, using perhaps the group brainstorming technique described in this section.
Alternatively, there are 'silly games' which can be played that have been invented by slightly absurd groups of adolescents. Titles of some we know are: 'Slobavian Football'; 'Dwile Flonking' and 'The Nubian Slave Game' - but that's all for a different book!

Returning to the edited highlights of 'Human Sacrifice', we think that you might want to volunteer some of your kids for some of these roles, or contrariwise, they might think of something for you!

HENGE

"The court is roughly circular in shape, 100 feet across, marked out by a ring of rough hewn stones weighing about 25 tons. Inside there is a circle of smaller stones and more big ones in a horseshoe shape. Outside the circle, some distance away, lies a slab called the Slaughter Stone, and it is here that, in the early sunshine

of Midsummer day the Old Sarum Fertility and Croquet club plays its annual game, Henge, or ritual murder".

"...Miss Gore Grimsby, the human sacrifice, sits in the centre of the horse shoe, laces up her running-pumps and ceremonially fastens the chinstrap of her May blossom wreath. Meanwhile, Mr Ron Priest, the Chairman of the Society and Wielder of the Sacrificial Implement, places his field where they can prevent the sacrifice from running away.

At the cry of 'Henge-up and Virgins Away', Miss Gore-Grimsby starts up and belts across the grass for the A303, where if she is lucky she will thumb a lift to the nearby Bulford camp and claim sanctuary from the British Army. If she does this, she is freed for life from being Sacrificial Victim, on the grounds that anyone who reaches Army Sanctuary is no longer considered eligible for Virgin Sacrifice. By carefully pacing her run, Miss Grimsby-Gore has managed to be caught and sacrificed every summer for the past 38 years."

FINGER LIFT

It is hard to describe the 'Finger Lift' without a diagram, so here goes!

The subject is seated and asked to relax. 4 levitators (group members) then use the forefingers of both hands to try and lift the subject. The lift points are under the thighs, behind the knees and under the armpits. Not too smelly, we hope!

On a pre-arranged signal, all the lifters use their two-fingered contact with the levitee (is there such a word?) and up the subject goes, but not very smoothly or very well. The subject is returned, gently to their chair, and at this point we include a touch of mysticism. Each lifter in a clockwise direction places one hand, palm downwards above the head of the person to be lifted. So, the hands at about 1" distance from one another form an 'aura of power' above the recipient's head until all 8 hands are displayed in this formation. Then slowly, one hand at a time from the top is withdrawn. The 4 lifters again take up positions using their two fore-fingers and this time miraculously, the person is lifted smoothly and easily and even 15 stone+ individuals 'float' towards the ceiling.

Don't ask us how or why it works this way, but work it does and all the participants get quite an electric buzz from the experience.

The exercise is best undertaken with teens' groups. From our experience, you may find yourself with a queue of eager participants and don't be too surprised if the staff members find themselves nearer the stars during the session in which the 'finger-lift' is tried out!

THE TRUTH GAME

There is more than one version of this 'heavy' sequence. It can be played in mixed adult/kids' groups, but we found that adults felt especially threatened by the exercise and in one conference we attended, two adult staff walked out of the group. The game can last for more than one 2 hour session or it can be scaled down to about an hour/hour and a half. It is useful if everyone can be given a stretch in the "hot seat" being questioned by the rest of the group.

To start, one person volunteers to be questioned. One question is asked of this person and they must then answer as truthfully as possible. At this point all the group can join in, asking **subsidiary** questions to the original. This process, when the game is played at its heaviest, continues until the whole group is satisfied that the question has been satisfactorily answered. The sequence then restarts with the last person who was interrogated being allowed to choose the new victim and pose the questions. Because the exercise relies on sharing one's personal life with the group, the level of aggression must be tempered with a high level of caring and sensitivity, making sure that everyone has made themselves vulnerable is one such means of ensuring that justice has been seen to be done.

The sort of questions which will inevitably be used will concern personal and sexual behaviour. Because of professional veneer and feelings of vulnerability, the adult participants in the group will be more likely to lie and misrepresent themselves. A strong (but participating) chairperson is needed!

Variations

A faster sequence, based on the same principle, is to use either cards or a 'one question rule' around the group. To amplify:

With cards

A pile of cards are placed in the middle of the group and each person in turn picks a card, reads it out and tries to answer truthfully. "What is the worst thing you've ever done?" is the sort of pro-forma. If a person cannot, or does not want to answer the question they have received, they can miss a turn.

Two or more sets of cards can be used, e.g. Personal, General, Work, School, etc., thus giving players the opportunity of choosing particular areas (and therefore the degree of threat).

Verbally

A volunteer starts by asking a question of the person on their left. That person answers, and then asks the person on their left a question and so on around the group. If someone says "pass" they forfeit their turn to ask a question.

THE RACK

The Rack is a very powerful sequence which should only be attempted with the most advanced small groups. It uses the adolescent's tendency to "slag" (criticise) his peers, and takes this to its limit. It is therefore unwise to attempt this sequence until such time as the group have discussed this tendency, and come to an awareness of the social contexts in which "slagging" takes place.

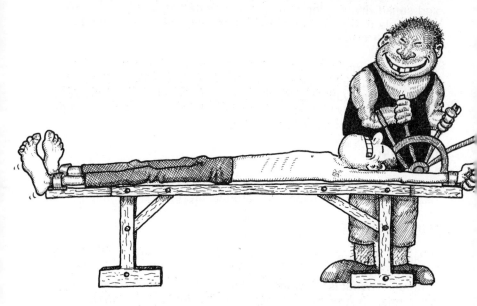

The person introducing the Rack should spend some time preparing the group for it, stressing that it is an exercise in self control which allows each individual to experience a whole range of negative feelings about them expressed by the rest of the group, in the knowledge that these do not outweigh the positive feelings.

Each person in the group (including the adults) takes it in turn to either sit in a chair in the centre of the circle, or lie stretched out on the floor. At a signal from the games leader, the person in the middle is put on the rack for a minute or a minute and a half. This involves the other group members trying every **verbal** thing they can think of to make the victim "crack". It is essential that the group spends time with each person immediately after they have been on the rack, discussing the feelings generated during the experience and whether or not it was found to be difficult.

"Rack-type" situations can arise spontaneously during the life of a group, and some workers will feel that they want to exploit this to the full. It is possible to introduce the Rack when this occurs as long as the group is at an appropriate stage of development.

However, bearing in mind the emotional stimulus that will have resulted in a spontaneous "rack" occurring, there is no guarantee that the experience will not backfire. Such spontaneous use is probably best left until the group have experienced, and are at ease with, the Rack.

THE GOOD AND THE BAD

A very demanding sequence which requires a high degree of trust and honesty between participants. It's use with a small group should be carefully planned and adults should note that this is a difficult sequence, even for an advanced group.

The sequence itself is very simple to organise. As an introduction, The Good and the Bad can be likened to the Truth Game, i.e. players must agree to tell the truth before the sequence commences. The "truth" element involves each person stating one thing they like about the person on their left, and one thing that they don't like.

Although a volunteer can be asked to start the sequence, it is particularly appropriate in this instance for an adult to go first, thus demonstrating that adults will be just as involved and honest as the kids. The games organiser's role is crucial in the Good and the Bad, as the onus is on him to "freeze" the game and invite group members to comment on a particular individual's statements - or to ask about feelings generated by specific comments. This quality of intervention demands an intimate knowledge of the group and its process.

Used sensitively, this sequence has much potential as long as workers are prepared to constructively use the material produced. Allow at least half an hour.

5 ethnic games

ETHNIC GAMES
DARTS

Darts is perhaps **the** standard pub game. It is also one of the traditional pieces of equipment possessed by most youth centres, alongside the table-tennis table and some form of snooker or pool table. Said to have been invented by two Royalist officers during the Civil War period and played in a convenient pub its ownership has also been claimed by Sussex folk, who in the 19th century were still playing "pug-darts", a game where a small dart was projected through a blow-pipe at a 4½ inch diameter board. Whatever its history, the game is now popular throughout Britain and except for a brief period in the 1940's when some Scottish magistrates tried to ban the game because they claimed that it encouraged "ne'er do wellism", the game has been well patronised by all sections of the community.

The game itself is played on what is usually a standard board, 18 inches in diameter with a set number sequence, 20 at the top, 3 at the bottom and with 'doubles' in a band at the outside of the scoring section of the board, a trebles band midway to the centre (or bull) and the centre 'inner' and 'outer' which score 50 and 25 respectively. Other boards exist in different localities, ranging from the Yorkshire board, with its single bull, no trebles and diamond shapes between the 14 and 9 and the 4 and 13, through to the London Target board with its concentric rings, which, like a bulls eye score 0-100 as the arrow approaches the centre of the board. The Target board and the Narrow Five board (where all numbers are multiples of five, i.e. 5, 10, 15 or 20; X1, X2, X3) are both used for games where players aim to reach a set score, say 1,000 first, unlike the traditional standard game of darts which is a reduction from 1001, 501 or 301 down to '0', with the final score having to be achieved exactly.

The distance away from the board varies, regionally from 8 ft, 8 ft 6 ins to 9 ft. But whichever distance is taken, the players are expected to 'toe the line' and not encroach over it.

There are other 'special' dart boards on the market, designed for playing particular games such as 'golf', and 'cricket', but our aim is to suggest a variety of games which can be played using the standard darts board as the basic equipment. For games on the dart board, we would suggest using one of the 'fun' introductions for choosing who starts first. If it is a singles game, nearest bull wins and if it is a pairs game the pairs are chosen by a process where all 4 players throw for bull and then the nearest and furthest away are paired, leaving the two middle players joined into the second team.

STANDARD DARTS

Tournament rules at a national level have been standardised, but the starting and finishing rules around the country vary.

To Start

After deciding whether the game is to be played in equal teams of more than 2 players a side, in pairs or singly, the starting total from which all subsequent scores are deducted, is established. As previously stated, this is normally 301, 501 or 1001.

In most places, play for an individual or team commences when they score a 'double'. From then on the aim is to reduce the starting score to zero in the fewest turns of 3 darts per go. Darts must remain sticking in the board for them to be counted and the player must toe the line for the go to be valid.

Scoring

If there is one available, the next challenger chalks the board and keeps score for the players either for one game or for a series of best of 3 games.

Finishing

When the player(s) reach a number of 50 or less that is a double of another number on the board, they aim for that double and if successful that throw takes them to zero and they win. If, however they miss, making their new total an odd number they continue until a new double is obtained. In most areas, if a player throws and goes past the number required, the score returns to the one at the beginning of the go.

So for example, a player aiming '40' who scores treble 20 returns to double top. In some areas, a 'no-bust' rule operates, meaning that if you find yourself going down from double 20, throw an odd number, say 21, leaving 19, you are not allowed to bust it to return to double 20 on the next turn. If you bust in this game you return to your last score, i.e. 19, or whatever, rather than the score from the beginning of the turn. When a player reaches double one (the lowest double) if he or she misses the double and hits a single one, many players will allow the thrower one dart to 'split the 11', meaning attempting to get a dart between the two legs of the 11. If the try is successful that player is adjudged to be the winner.

ROUND THE CLOCK

This is a singles game for any number of players. Everyone starts by aiming at No. 1 and then for No. 2 in order through to 20 or even to 50 (the bull). Usually an extra throw is allowed for players who score the number that they aim for with the last dart (third).

It is a useful introduction to the position of numbers on the board and not too difficult for the beginner. Whether you allow doubles and trebles to count is a question of 'local rules'.

For a more advanced game, you can play all the way round on doubles and/or only allow an extra go if all three darts 'scored'.

KILLER

This is one of the most popular alternative games for use on the dartboard. It is also one of the most fiendish, since the aim is to knock opponents off the board completely. If used in an I.T. group one must be careful that resentment does not run too high! It is a game for groups of 4 or more, so it fits the group work model well in terms of size if not in ethos.

To start, players throw one dart each with the hand they don't normally use, until they hit a number. That is then their number (unless it is already occupied) through until the end of the game. Normally the game is then played using the normal hand thus:

1) Each player tries to get exactly 5 of his or her number. (Doubles count X2; trebles X3).

2) If a surplus is scored you reduce the score by the extra i.e. if, when on 4 threes you hit a treble 3, the score goes up 1 and down 2, so the end result is 3 threes, one down on the start.

3) Once a player has 5 of their number they are marked up as killer, which is normally written as 1111K. They can then aim for any opponents' numbers. If the person they hit is killing, that person must then aim for their own number again before they are killer again.

Numbers must be killed off exactly, or otherwise lives are given back.

4) If non-killers hit other players' numbers, apart from those killing, they can give lives to the opposition.

5) The winner is the last player left in.

There are a number of variations of this game, but this is the one we like best. Obviously, the game can be played using less lives, such that only '3' of a number are required to become killer. On the other end of the scale, the game could be revised using 'doubles' only - so 3 doubles for instance are needed before a person is killing.

SCRAM

Is played by two players. One player acts as "STOPPER", the other is "SCORER". Stopper throws first, normally aiming at the highest numbers first. (Bull is not used). These numbers are counted as 'dead' once hit by the Stopper. The Scorer must then aim for other parts of the board and score the maximum points. Trebles and Doubles count. The game goes on until all numbers have been hit by the Stopper; the Scorer's total is fixed and roles reversed. The winner is the person who scores most as Scorer.

MICKEY MOUSE

The first requirement of this game is to chalk up a run of numbers on the blackboard e.g.

A				B
	111	20	111	
	111	19	111	
	111	18	111	
Score	111	17	111	Score
	111	16	111	
	111	15	111	
	111	14	111	
	111	13	111	
	111	12	111	
	111	11	111	
	111	10	111	
Total =	111	B	111	Total =

The marks to the left and right of the numbers represent the number of times each player has 'hit' the number in question (doubles and trebles count as 2X and 3X respectively). Once a player has 3 of a number, they are scoring on that number until the

opponent 'closes' the number by getting their 3 of that number.

The game ends when all the numbers are closed and the winner is the player with the highest total.

This works best with players who are fairly used to playing darts or who are at the same standard of play.

FIVES

A very simple game which can be fun and doesn't require great skill. Any number from 2 upwards can play. Each player throws 3 darts and must have all 3 darts in the scoring part of the board. The aim is to score a total which is divisable by 5, then that number i.e. $40 \div 5 = 8$ is scored. Play continues up to a pre-arranged total, normally 50 or 61. Scores not divisable by 5 are worthless. You can vary the game by scoring on numbers divisable by 5 and 3 which is perhaps easier with kids, although the scoring becomes more difficult. Thus 15 would score on 3's and 5's which gives $(15 \div 3 = 5) + (15 \div 5 = 3) = 8$ total.

DARTS
FOOTBALL

The name of this game should appeal to all the male youth club/group members. How's that for chauvinism? There are various versions, all normally for two or for teams. The one we like best is a variant of 'Round-the-Clock'. Players choose whether their goal is No. 1 or No. 20. Then, after the toss of a coin (well, it is football!) one side kicks off. This is done by aiming at 11 if the player's goal is 1 and 10 if the goal is 20. From then on play proceeds up and down the number range of the board.

PLAYER A   **PLAYER B**

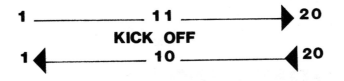

If, for instance, Player A scores 11 with the first dart, misses with the second and hits 12 (his direction of play) with the third, the player goes again, **third dart scoring** meaning an extra go. Perhaps, only the second dart finds the 13 target in this go, so at this point play changes to Player B, who tries to move the ball in the opposite direction i.e. towards Player A's goal at No. 1. Player B **must** aim at the last number successfully hit by Player A, thus he or she takes up the ball by hitting point 13 and then aims for 12, 11, and so on in descending order. Play continues until a goal is scored, then another kick-off takes place.

As a game it is good practice and can be an absorbing way of spending half an hour.

Alternatives are: Each player aims at the bull/inner. Success gives control of the ball, allowing that player to shoot at doubles (goal). Each double is one goal and this barrage continues until the opponent regains possession by scoring a bull. Normally a ten goal limit determines the end of the game.

A strange 3rd variety of football is for experts only. Players aim for a number and once this has been determined, (They must both be different) each player shoots for a progression of segments. This is most easily explained in a diagram:

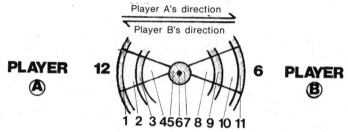

Key

Small numbers (1) etc. indicate ..e direction of play and segments which must be hit by Player (A) on the way towards Player (B)'s goal at double 6. Player (B)'s play is the exact reverse.

The first player to achieve all hits at every segment en route is the winner. The 'third dart hit carries on' can be used.

BURMA ROAD

This is one of the 'greats' we think in the kids' group situation. It can be played with large groups which is often a godsend, if the dartboard has suddenly become a popular place. First, a series of arbitrary numbers is chosen, normally including double, treble, bull and possibly a 'nominated name'. Each player then aims for each number or segment in turn. The scoreboard provides a clear explanation of what is happening - if a player fails to score with any of the 3 darts, the cumulative total is halved (odd numbers count high).

A	B		C	D	E
20	—	20	20	40	100
10	2	2	22	44	102
16	59	T	11	22	129
20	63	4	31	26	65
35	93	15	106	13	80
75	99	D	53	39	40
81	123	6	59	45	20
121	143	Nom.	78	65	140
130	72	9	39	83	149
65	36	B	89	42	75

As you can see from the score sheet the game has skillful elements, but the lead can change very fast and the end is frequently a surprise, even to the myopic 7 year old who has just beaten the youth club leader who fancies himself a bit!

A rule that can be included is to say that all players must make some score in   one   of the first 3 rounds. Linked to this, the player who has reached a score of 1, stays put for 3 rounds before being eliminated.

SHANGHAI

This is a popular game and the technical meaning of 'Shanghai' sometimes spills over into the Standard 301-type game. Shanghai is to score a single, treble and double of any number in the same 3 darts. This can be used as an end game in standard darts if all contestants are agreed. It adds, like the 'split the 11' rule an extra fun element. If used in 301, it must be 'called' before the third dart is thrown.

Anyway in this game a board is marked up.

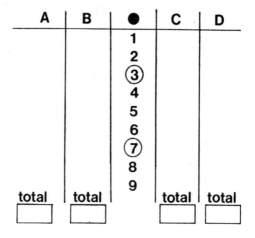

Each player throws 3 darts at each number in order scoring the total. Doubles and Trebles count. 3's and 7's must be scored (if you are playing the 'serious' game) - failure means dropping out.

A Shanghai (double, treble, single) on the other hand means outright victory.
Otherwise the player with the highest total wins.

This is a good game for groups of players, but perhaps the ' 3' and '7' drop out numbers - known as being 'Shanghaied' needs omitting with kids' groups.

DARTS
CRICKET

This can be played by 2 players, or teams. One side 'bats', the other 'bowls'. In the version we prefer, the batting team scores as runs, everything scored above 40 (but they must not hit the inner or outer bull).

The bowlers try to hit the bull - inner counts two innings (i.e. two batsmen out) and an outer as one off. The scoreboard looks like:

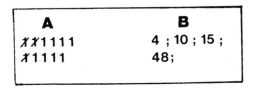

A	B
X̶X̶1111	4 ; 10 ; 15 ;
X̶1111	48;

At this point the score is 77 runs for 3 wickets.

After an innings, i.e. 11 or 10 wickets have fallen, sides reverse roles and at the end of one or two innings for each side a victor is found.

Not a bad game, but it requires some skill from the bowlers, which can make it rather slow!

One additional rule which we have seen used is to count as runs to the batting team darts thrown by the bowling team which end up outside the treble ring. This gives just an ever so slight incentive to the bowlers to achieve accurate results!

NOUGHTS AND
CROSSES

If you want a game that is easy to explain and immediately appeals to youngsters, try this one! The noughts and crosses grid is drawn up with numbers from the darts board written in to the squares. It's for 2 players or teams of equal numbers.

1	2	3
4	5	6
7	8	9

Players either aim for 'singles' of each number, or for more interest value, 'doubles' of the numbers concerned. As numbers are hit, the numbers are replaced by noughts and crosses. Thus:

X	X	0
4	5	0
X	8	0

With the '0' player having scored on 3, 6 & 9. A more advanced version can be played using the Bull (inner or outer) for the centre squares. So that the grid becomes (i.e.)

17	2	4
11	B	5
9	3	20

DOMINOES

If you didn't know it, there are not always 28 dominoes (stones, blocks, tiles or bones) in a pack. The set beginning with a double blank and running through all the possibilities to double six is the most common, but you may stumble across any size of pack up to double twelves, which would give you 91 tiles - rather a large number for the normal coffee table!

Anyway, we have assumed that you are the proud possessors of the double-six pack and that you have always been afraid of displaying your singular lack of knowledge in front of the youngsters.

Games can be played by anything from 2 upwards. If 'partnerships' are involved then they can be decided by agreement or by drawing from the pack. The two players with the 'heaviest' dominoes (i.e. the highest numerical value) then form a pair. Partners normally sit opposite each other. Play proceeds with each player following on with matching dominoes corresponding with the number at one or other end of the line. We are not convinced that it is the best of all group games, therefore we only include a limited variety of alternatives. However, having said that, if you ever work with a West Indian group, you will have to learn their variety of domino games.

THE BASIC GAME

BLOCK DOMINOES

This is what 301 is, to darts. The aim is to be the first person to get rid of all the dominoes. With 2 players, each take seven tiles; 3 or 4 players take either five or six of the blocks. The other dominoes are left aside in what is usually called the 'Boneyard'. Normally, if convention matters, this drawing of dominoes from the face-down assortment on the table is done in rotation. The person who has drawn the 'heaviest' domino prior to the start of the game starts proceedings by laying a domino on the table. (In some areas the starting domino will be the highest double in anyone's hand. This rather than a previous draw would then determine the person to commence). In doubles play this will indicate to the partner which suit (i.e. numbers) may be preferred.

Play continues around the table until a player can't go. He or she indicates this by 'knocking' the table. All doubles are played across the line of dominoes and not lengthways:

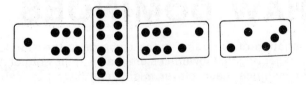

In most games someone will manage to get rid of all their dominoes. Where this doesn't occur, play ends when all the players can't go. The total of the 'pips' on the players' tiles are scored at the end of each round and a final limit of, say 100 or 200 is set. The person with the lowest score at the time when someone reaches the total is declared the winner.

A VARIATION ON THE THEME

This game is exactly the same **except that** players may put on the table as many tiles as they wish in each go, as long as they join by numbers. So, the person commencing might lay down five dominoes, leaving only one. Player 2, could then put down only two and Player 3 is blocked by Player 2 "closing-off" each end with the same number.

A hint which is useful for all new players is that they should try to get rid of all their 'heavy' tiles first, thereby avoiding the risks of being caught with a high score.

With both the traditional games, we found that they worked best with younger children under twelve and were better in the singles versions, rather than in pairs. At least a few squabbles were avoided.

In pairs' games there are a couple of other rules;

(1) The winner of the previous hand starts.

(2) Pairs score jointly; as soon as one of the pair are out they score all the pips left. Some domino games are played where both partners must get out for their side to win.

The game **can** catch the imagination of youngsters, or at least their liking for the mundane and repetitive. At other times it may be best to pass immediately on to what we view as a more interesting game before putting the kids off the use of dominoes.

DRAW DOMINOES

This variation of the game is the same as in the standard block game, excepting that fewer tiles are drawn at the start of the game. So, for instance, each player might only have five 'cards' each. When a person is blocked they then draw from the pool of the 'boneyard'. This style of playing can be "attached" to almost any of the games, usually ensuring that a conclusion of some one going out is reached.

FIVES AND THREES

Requiring a wee bit of brain-work, this game offers more variety for players and was a firm favourite with some of our groups. It is a combination of 3 other games, known as Muggins, all-fives and all-threes. With 2, 3 or 4 players, each draws 6 tiles.

A player leads with any domino - but the aim is to place tiles which add up to a number divisible by 3 or 5, or even both, like 15. For instance, if the first player puts down a double six, they score 12 ÷ 3 = 4 points. In the example below:

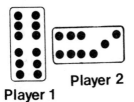

Player 1 **Player 2**

the second player makes a total of 15, double-six plus a three at the other end of the line. This gives that player a score of 8; 15 ÷ 3 = 5 and 15 ÷ 5 = 3; 5 + 3 = 8. A cribbage board is useful for scoring, marking up the points as they are gained.

The game is played up to 31 or 61 and the **exact** number must be achieved. This will probably take 3 or 4 hands - about the right length of play for youngsters. The partnership game can be played, as with the standard game, either by having one or both players using up all their tiles. Singles play ends, obviously when a player uses the last block, or when everyone cannot go.

ST ANDREW'S CROSS

Could this be Scottish? Well we tried for a touch of "north of the border", didn't we? With 4 players, this game is based on a double-four lead. Each player draws six tiles until someone can play this double-four lead. There are only 4 'sleepers' in the boneyard, so it shouldn't take too long. From these bases as can be seen in the diagram, each player has their 'own' line, lettered A, B, C, & D.

135

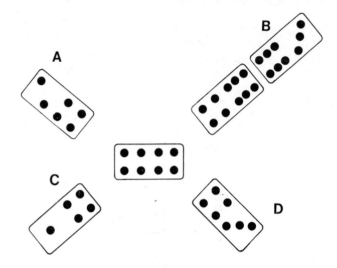

Play proceeds in the normal way, one tile each but **only** on their own line. If a player is 'blocked' and knocks, the next player in sequence can play on the blocked players' line **and** their own, thus getting rid of two dominoes in a turn. The game ends when a player goes out or the game is blocked, so no-one can go. Spots are totalled etc.

BERGEN

We found that this was fun, challenging and rewarding. It is a combination of the essence of various other games. The aim is for the 2,3 or 4 players to be the first out, but there is also a strong element of blocking - giving the kids a chance to be aggressive, and point scoring to allow them to amass wealth. Just like life! If a player can make the two ends have the same number they score 2 points. Playing a double to make both ends the same, scores 3 points. Playing against a double also gives 3 points. By this we mean, adding a new block onto a double which gives the same number as at the other end i.e.

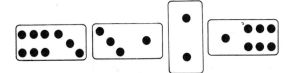

Placing the 1 and 6 gives a 3 score.

The start of the game is with 6 dominoes for 2 or 3 players and 5 tiles for 4 players. The highest double starts and players unable or unwilling to add to the sequence must draw from the boneyard.

A player getting rid of their final domino also scores 2 points.

Game score is normally 15.

Altogether it is different enough to appeal to newcomers and old-hands at the game.

MATADOR

Again, this is unusual. With 2 players, each takes 7 dominoes, for 3 it is 6 and with 4 players, 5 blocks each. The highest double normally starts and the participants try to get rid of their pieces. Doubles are placed in line instead of across the row. Matadors are dominoes which total '7'. A 6 and 1; 5 and 2; 4 and 3 plus the 0/0 blank.

In the version we like and used, there is no need to follow numbers i.e. 3 to a 3. Rather, players must make the join add up to 7. So:

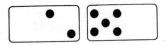

is a successful play.

Alternatively, a matador may be played, which will be played across the line i.e.

To follow this, a 2 or 5 join will be needed to create the lucky 7 total, or another Matador in which case the matador will be played with the line rather than across. Players unable to go (or unwilling) draw one from the boneyard.

The game can be scored, by counting 1 point per join or Matador. The player who plays all his or her dominoes first receives one point for each pip on opponents' blocks. If it is a blocked game, it is the person with the lowest value on their dominoes who wins their adversaries' points, minus the value of their own residue.

101 is the normal winning total.

This game is normally especially appreciated as a spice of variety by older groups. Surprisingly, even staff have been known to enjoy playing!

BLIND HUGHIE

One supposes that any section should have an idiotic, "silly" game. This is it! it is also Scottish, originating with 'slightly' worse for wear Fifeshire miners. Between 2 and 5 maniacs are required and each draws 5 blocks. No player looks at the blocks and all are lined up in front of the individuals concerned. Player One turns over the block on the left of the line and places it in the centre of the table. Player Two turns over his similar domino and if it matches block 1, it is played in the normal way. If it doesn't it is placed, face upwards at the right hand end of the player's line of blocks.

It all helps to get the dominoes back into their box at the end of the session!

SEBASTAPOL

This is a variant of the standard game and not particularly exceptional, although quite widely played. The double six is led (or found in the boneyard pool and laid on the table). Each player draws seven dominoes and play

must be made in all 4 directions as in the diagram off the double-six **before** any further progress is made.

Apart from this and the 4 points of play, the only additional way in which Sebastapol varies from the Block game is in not placing other doubles across the line. They are played like any other block and no more than 4 open ends are allowed.

All we can say is that it makes a pretty pattern, but the liking or otherwise of the game depends on your feelings towards the basic game.

POOL

In Britain, pool has 'taken over' from the traditional games of snooker, billiards and bar-billiards. The species of pool played almost universally is so standard as not to be worth repeating. It is best known as 'eight ball pool' because the black 8 ball is the last to be pocketed, each player or team potting either spots (solid coloured balls) or stripes and then pot black. The only variations which may add to the games which you play with youth groups are concerning the end game, i.e. potting the black. Regretably, the full game of pool cannot be played on most tables because they have 'sealed' pockets and have different markings.

1)   The standard game is to nominate which pocket the black ball is aimed for and that player is only the winner if the ball is successfully potted in that pocket.

2)   An 'alternative' and easier end game is simply potting the black without nomination.

3)   "Last Bag". This one is more fun and skillful. Whichever pocket a player's ball goes in becomes 'their pocket' for the black. If the game is level, this can make for an exciting and frustrating chase of cat and dog up and down the board. Players may not have the same pocket and if this does occur the second player's home-base is the one opposite, either diagonally or horizontally.

4)   Much the same as in version 3, but it is the first ball into the pocket from each player that establishes the pocket for the end game. A useful tip to aid a decaying memory is to put a "marker" by the respective pockets.

5) Potting the black ball can be made much more nerve-racking by stipulating that since both players are 'on the black', a foul stroke loses the game.

A source of some disagreement in all the pool-type games concerns whether an 'extra shot' given after a foul stroke is 'carried on.' By this, we mean, if Player A miscues and misses all the balls, 2 strokes are allowed for Player B. In question, is what happens if Player B pots a ball, do they still have 2 strokes? Some say yes, some no. We sit on the fence, but it is worthwhile knowing in advance that you may be required to adjudicate.

Pool doesn't much lend itself to alternative games, not at least of a type that a youth worker would want to encourage. The main one we know and has proved successful and popular is ROTATION.

ROTATION

The balls are set out as in diagram:

Players both start by aiming at the ball numbered no. 1.

They are trying to pot it, or hit the 1 ball and rebound on to a higher value ball striking it into a pocket i.e.

THE REBOUND SHOT

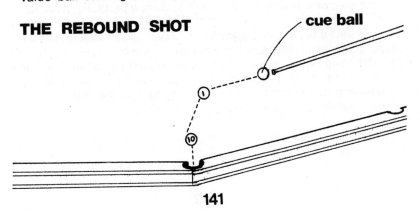

It's a sort of combination of pool and billiards. Scoring is achieved by potting the balls, either in strict order - rotation 1, 2, 3, 4, etc. or by rebound shots, which obviously allow for rapid scoring. A successful 'pot' gives the player an additional shot, as with most other games of this type. We used a two shot penalty or a 2 point penalty for foul shots:-

i.e.   (1)   missing all the balls
           (2)   hitting a wrong ball
           (3)   potting a wrong ball

The winner is the player with the highest score, when all the balls have disappeared (preferably inside the machine!) from sight.

POOL GOLF

This game cannot be played on a pool table unless the coin mechanism is set to automatically return the balls. Because accurate potting is important, we found after a boring half an hour that the game does **not** easily transfer over to a scaled-down snooker table. Anyway, returning to the pool table the first player selects one ball to act as club and one as ball for a 'round' of golf. Each player has their own club and their own ball for the duration of the game - an easy(ish) way to remember whose ball belongs to which player is to arrange it so that 'spots' are the golf balls and 'stripes' the clubs. If these are paired off according to colour, they are readily identifiable.

The golf ball is placed on the top of table spot and the club in the 'D'. A 1st hole is chosen and that is the target with cue being applied to club ball and that hitting the ball. Each player proceeds in this way, one stroke at a time and scoring a particular number of shots per hole en route. This continues with each player shooting in turn until a ball is potted, then that player goes again for the next hole, playing clockwise around the table. Each pocket represents a hole, and once around the table represents a six-hole golf competition. If you don't want to remember how many strokes have been taken, the game can be played with the first person to finish (as in pool) being declared the winner.

Penalties

When a player pots either of their balls by mistake this gives a penalty of "losing one hole" and that player shoots again for the previous pocket.

When a player pots an opposing player's ball, they return to the previous hole.

Missing your own ball did not incur any penalty in the version we played, nor did hitting an opponent's ball without potting it.

Overall, it's quite a popular game as long as there are not more than three players. Two can be even better since the pace of the game is increased.

RACING

Ideally for this game, you need a pool table where you will not have to pay.

It's a 'one-at-a-time' game, each person playing against the clock. One ball, it doesn't matter what colour or value, is placed on the spot at the top of the table and the white cue ball is placed in the D. The player tries to pot the ball at the top of the table. Whether this effort is successful or otherwise, the result is the same. Another ball is brought up as a new **cue ball**, again regardless of what it is. Within a two minute period or whatever limit is set, the player scores one point for each ball potted. Once you have run out of "cue balls", you have to stop even if you are still within the time limit. Any number can compete and it allows plenty of opportunity for kids to try out their new digital watches with the seconds read out.

At the end of a round, the player with the highest score wins.

SIDES

Played as in the standard 8-ball game, with one side taking spots and the other, stripes, there is an extra difference indicated by which **side** of the table the first ball goes down. That side is then the player's personal domain and all that player's balls must be potted in the 3 pockets along that side. Failure to do so, incurs the standard 2 stroke penalty. The black ball end game can be played in a number of ways, but normally the black **must** be potted in one of the pockets nominated on the player's side of the table.

A good game to vary the monotony and one which requires an extra degree of skill - so it should preferably be introduced with youngsters who have mastered the standard game.

CARD GAMES

There, are literally thousands of games using a pack or packs of cards. We are not intending even the slightest attempt at comprehensive coverage. Instead we have selected games which youngsters have subjected us to with surprisingly pleasing results and games with which we have returned the compliment.

Games with cards fall into two distinct categories for our purposes and then those games may be further sub-divided. Some are primarily games of chance; others rely on a range of skills: memory, careful timing and/or good partnership. We were surprised how many of the kids we played with were not used to even 'standard' games such as Knockout Whist. That one we include, whilst most of the others in this section are 'fun' games aimed at involvement rather than sorting out potential Einstein's. Many are quite noisy, so don't go thinking that card games are automatically destined for the quiet room! We hope that you find a few gems which you can use with your youth groups. There aren't many games included which are going to reduce the loose change in your pocket!

SWITCH

A highly ritualised version of this was introduced to us by a group of outgoing girls in a youth club. It is a game largely of chance and a round can last some time - but it's fun and **is** distinctly odd!

Each player is dealt seven cards. The top card is turned over, and the player to the left of the dealer has a range of choices.

A player may:
1) follow suit (i.e. club on club)
2) follow number (i.e. 5 on 5)
3) Play an ace, which can be played anytime and allows the player to choose a new suit.

Other cards have peculiar powers as well.

A QUEEN reverses the order of play and allows the player to put down an additional card. (i.e. left or right direction). A TWO played means that the **next** player must pick up two cards from the pack and miss a go (another TWO may be played by the following player in which case four cards must be picked up by the next player, and so on). A SIX is the really weird card! This leads to a SWITCH, not of direction but of total hand i.e. a six is played and everyone must pass on all their cards to the next person in the direction of play. Players who cannot go, pick up one card.

The only other rule concerns players when there is only one card left in their hand. They must announce the fact. Failure brings a penalty of one pick-up card. Very annoying to the recipient. The winner is the first person to get rid of all the cards. Altogether quite entertaining.

GO FISHING

"Lively and different", as they say in all promotional blurbs. "Go Fishing" we have played with groups of up to 5 players. In these cases, each individual is dealt 9 cards. For more than 5, only 8 or even 7 cards are distributed, otherwise there will not be any pack for 'pick-ups'.

The Dealer starts and play continues in a clockwise direction. In a turn, player A asks any other individual for cards of a certain value, say, for instance a player has at least one six they may ask Player C for sixes and receive two. A player may only ask for cards of any value, if they hold at least one of the type in their hand. But, when they are successful in obtaining, say, sixes from a player, they may then: (a) ask the same player for cards of another value or (b) ask another player for some particular cards.

When asked, a player must hand over **all** the cards of a particular value.

A turn ends when a player has failed to 'find' the card/cards which they are seeking. The player then picks up the top card from the pack. If this card is of the same denomination as the one asked for, the player continues. When a player fails to find the cards sought, the turn ends and a card is picked up. Play then moves on to the turn of the next player in a clockwise direction.

The aim is to make sets of 4 which are immediately put down on the table. Any set of 4 cards scores 40 points, except aces, which score 60 points. If a player runs out of cards, he or she must pick up a card from the pack; if no cards are left then that player totals up their score and drops out of the game.

The game ends when every set is on the table. The person with the most points at the end wins, or in the case of a draw, players enter into a novel end game of a TIEBREAK, which is:

"The players involved shuffle the pack and a cut is made. Then each player in turn takes the top card and this continues until one draws an ace. That player is the eventual winner."

RACING DEMON

This is admirably crazy and if tempers don't get too frayed it works as an ideal game for groups of youngsters. It can be played by two or more. That is perhaps one of the only problems - if it is possible it is best to avoid the kids getting over involved and highly strung. Anyway, at best it is a lot of fun, fast and frantic. To save that family heirloom of a pack of cards we recommend only using old packs, complete, but without jokers. **One pack is needed per player** and plenty of room for spreading out. Being alert is the main requirement, so an advantage we would proclaim for Racing Demon is that it can be played by a mixed age range. Beware brothers and sisters who like thumping one another!

Each player shuffles his or her own pack, then 13 cards are dealt into a pile and the pile is left face upwards. Besides this a row of four face upward cards are dealt. Each player is left with a pack of "leftovers" which they clutch in their hand. The aim of the game is rather like a 'competitive patience' race game. All are trying to get rid of their pile of 13 cards and move out cards from the 4 separate piles. They do this, after the word "go" has been uttered.

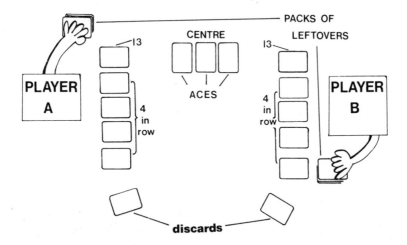

There is no order of play after the word "go", so for starters, all players move any aces they have into the centre area, to which all players may add in suit sequence in ascending order (Ace low). They should then replenish the 4 piles, by moving the top card from the pile of 13. Cards may also be moved from the top of any of the 4 piles into the centre area, remembering that players must follow suit. The piles of 4 operate in descending order and alternate red and black cards must be played.

If a player cannot move one of the top cards from the '4 piles' or the '13 piles' then they may take 3 cards from the top of the pack of "leftovers" and play any one at a time onto the centre piles or onto the '4 piles'. Any not used are put in a discard pile, face up. A fourth type of move involves shifting all, or part of one of the '4 piles' onto one of the player's other '4 piles'. The advantage of this

147

Play to
CENTRE
e.g. all hearts

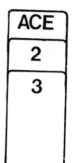

Play on
FACE-UP
ROW OF 4

E.G.

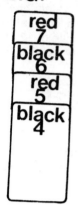

DIAGRAM 2

move is that it may allow a card to be uncovered that can be moved into the 'centre' or it may create a space in the '4 piles' which will allow the top card from the '13 piles' to be moved across to fill the gap.

That's about it. It sounds complicated, but in fact it is really easy to learn. The result is a mad scramble which can be lots of fun. Remember, that quick action moving into the 'Centre' will block opponents and may win the game.

Once any player uses up all the cards in the '13 piles' they say 'out' and play ceases.

The scoring is unique and explains why cards should be moved into the 'centre' as quickly as possible. Each player counts up all the cards left in the 13 and 4 piles. Then the cards in the centre are divided up into piles one for each player. This is easy because each has a distinctive pack.

For instance.

PLAYER	1	2	3
IN 4 AND 13 PILES	13	5	12
IN CENTRE	30	32	14
SCORE	(-13) 17	(-5) 27	(-12) 2

If you are responsible for a group playing this game it is quite advisable that you explain the rules and then referee. It can develop into quite a fight!

A recap of the moves each player may be making, in order of priority.

(1) move aces to Centre
(2) move any card from 4 or 13 piles to Centre
(3) move the top card from 13 pile to 4 pile
(4) move cards from one pile to another
(5) pick up top 3 cards from 'leftover' pack and play any into Centre or piles
(6) discard face up, any from move (5) and when the "leftover" pack in hand is finished the discards are picked up, turned face down and held as the "leftovers".

KNOCKOUT WHIST

The most "common" of the games we have included. It is still a proven success.

It can be played with between 3 and 7 players. With any number of players, 7 cards are dealt to each and the top card of the remainder is turned over. For the first hand this dictates the Trump suit.

The player to the dealer's left leads and other players follow suit if they can, or trump or discard to the lead if they don't have any cards of the correct suit. Tricks are kept by individual players and the highest number of tricks won allows that player to choose trumps in the next hand.

After the round with 7 cards, the sequence is repeated with 6 cards and then 5 and so on down to 1. If any player fails to win a trick they then receive 1 card in the following hand which they can play at any time during that hand. If they win a trick they are back in the game. For obvious reasons, this extra 'life' does not take place after the two or one card hands! Players who have failed to make a 'trick' in these hands are well and truly "knocked out".

ROCKAWAY

This combines fun and lunacy with some level of skill. It's easy enough to learn, yet reasonably satisfying for all the players. Any number can play and almost any age group.

Seven cards are dealt to each player face downwards and one card is placed face upwards in the centre of the table - this is known as the "Kitty". All discards are placed onto this kitty throughout the game.

The aim is to be the first player to get rid of all the cards in the hand. This is done simply by discarding onto the Kitty, following either

> THE SUIT (i.e. diamonds)
> THE NUMBER (i.e. 5)
> or PLAYING AN ACE (which are wild and can only
> be followed by another ace
> or a card of the same suit).

Skill is shown in careful planning of the discards. Ace should not be played unless necessary. If a player cannot go, they must draw from the remainder of the pack which has been placed face downwards on the table. After the pack runs out, players miss a turn only if they cannot go.

The winner plays his or her last card onto the discard and then the score is totalled up **against** the other individuals:

ACE scores 15
COURT cards 10
Other cards face value

It's quite fun, reasonably active and not quite so hard to supervise as racing demon.

BLACKOUT

Simplicity itself, Blackout is played with between 3 and 7 players.

Some cards are discarded from the pack, but not exposed, depending on the number of players

	TRICKS
With 3 players 1 card is left	17
With 4 the whole pack is used	13
With 5 players 2 cards are left out	10
With 6 players 4 cards are left out	8
With 7 players 3 cards are left out	7

The whole pack is dealt out, with the last card to the dealers hand being exposed - this is then the TRUMP SUIT. The person on the dealer's left now says how many tricks they hope to make and this continues around the table. Say, with 4 players, these calls might be: (out of a possible 13 tricks)

PLAYER A	7
PLAYER B	4
PLAYER C	2
PLAYER D	2
	15

The last player to bid **must not** make a bid which, taken together with the other bids adds up to the correct number of tricks for the game.

Play then commences, as in whist. The player to the left of the dealer leads and when that 'trick' has been won, the winner leads.

Suits led must be followed if possible, otherwise they can be trumped or cards can be 'thrown'.

At the end of a round the tricks are scored at 1 point each with 10 point bonuses for any players making the correct number. A total of 50 or a 100 can be taken at end of game.

A competitive and clever game.

PELMANISM

Not really a card game, more a game with cards if you can make the distinction. Played even with young groups of players, pelmanism is easy to learn and a good test of memory. We noticed that the older the players, the worse they were - I wonder what that means? Later in the book we comment on "Baffle Box" which is virtually a commercial version of part of the same idea.

Any number can play and one or two packs are spread out, face down over the table. You need a rather large space, since the whole pack is distributed. Once the cards are on the table, there must be enough room between them, so that cards are not touching, they must remain in the same positions even after being turned over.

The idea is to collect pairs, turning over two cards randomly at a time - if they are a pair then the player keeps removing them from the playing area. If they are not a pair, they are turned back over in the same spaces. A player who finds a pair continues to look at two cards until they fail in their quest. Play continues with each player searching for pairs in the same way.

The winner is the player with the most pairs at the end of the game. Boring for adults or perhaps embarrassing?

MINORU or THE DERBY

If spending lunchtimes in the Betting Office is your I.T. group's favourite pastime this is the ideal game. You need some counters since the game simulates a horse race and the gambling which precedes it.

First mark out a large sheet of paper, as follows:

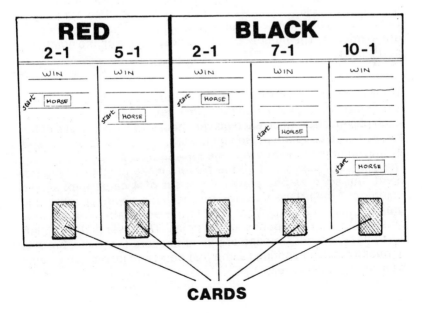

Stakes, i.e. counters are then placed above the columns and the person acting as banker keeps an eye on proceedings.

The race starts: 5 cards are dealt, face downwards onto the spaces at the botom of the columns. These are the 'horses'. Below these, five cards are dealt face upwards. The horse with the highest card gets a move one column up the course. The race continues with cards being dealt until a horse reaches the top line - the finishing post.

The odds are correct mathematically, with a slight advantage for the banker. We suggest that each player takes 4 turns as banker before passing on the bank. Players may also bet on 'red' or 'black' - the banker pays even money.

Happy horse racing - it will probably supply ideas for the next group outing in the mini-bus!

SPOONS

Our name for a furious, noise-filled bit of nonsense, which is a card party game. Like 'Pelmanism' it's ideal with young groups, or a wide age-range. The slightly 'special' equipment required is spoons, one less in number than the players and an old pack of cards from which sets of 4 (of a kind, kings or aces for example) are extracted. The number of sets corresponds with the number of participants.

The spoons are placed in the centre of the table at the beginning of the game. Play involves shuffling the sets of cards, dealing 4 to each player, after which each player chooses a card from his or her hand to pass on to the person on the left. All the cards are passed, at the same time face down. The new cards are looked at, a new "pass-on" is chosen and all the players make another change of hand. As soon as one player has a set of 4 cards they should quietly put them face upwards on the table shout 'spoons!' and grab a spoon. Other players have to pay some attention, for they must also reach for spoons at this point. The loser is the one left 'spoonless'. Various means are used to score the game, but it is normally negative-scoring i.e. the first person to lose 6 games may have to perform forfeit.

It is the sort of game, which, if used in a session of 'heavier' and 'lighter' experiences is an excellent tension breaker.

SEQUENCE

Groups of 4 or 5 are best for this game, but 2 or more can play. The aim is to get rid of cards before the opponents. All the cards are dealt out between the players. The player on the dealer's left puts down on the table the lowest card (2's count lowest; Ace high) in their hand and the player with the next card must follow the sequence i.e. the 2 of hearts would be followed by the three of the same suit. The sequence continues until the ace is played. At this point the player of the ace plays any card of their choice. The sequence continues until the Ace is reached, or where a suit has been used before up to the highest card left to be played. The following sequence is then started by the person who played the last card. The winner is the person to play all their cards first.

If more than one round is required, then a scoring system can be devised, say for instance, the first player to win 3 rounds is the overall champion of Sequence.

The playing of the sequence 'starter' cards is quite skillful and staff won't mind participating too much. We found that this game was rather contagious and we were still suffering outbreaks weeks after the game was introduced.

SHOVE HA'PENNY

An English contrivance first used in pubs, it can be made of wood or slate and the size, if you were thinking of making your own is 2 ft long by 1 ft 2" wide with the grain running lengthwise. Often the top end of the board has a semi-circular raised edge to prevent the ha'pennies going over the top end. Ten lines (grooves) in the board run horizontally across the table and each of the nine beds are 1¼" wide. Squares on each side of the beds, divided by a vertical groove provide space for chalking in each player's score. This is normally done by marking two horizontal lines 11 and then when the player's bed is full a third line strikes through thus, ̶1̶1̶.

The game has limited appeal with youth groups but can be a valued piece of equipment if used intelligently. However, it is unlikely to compete for popularity with the pool table. Each player has five discs to "shove" up the board with palm of hand, thumb or tips of fingers - all are legal. The aim is get three ha'pennies in each of the nine beds. Coins overlapping the lines in any way are adjudged 'out'. Normally coins which cross the first line are in play, otherwise if the ha'penny is mis-hit and **hasn't** hit another coin or touched the first line, they can be taken back to the beginning of the board and restruck. Once a player has 3 in a bed it is viewed as full and if that player shoves another coin into the bed, and the opponent has not filled up the bed then that other player receives a bonus 'credit' - one point for each coin so misplaced.

The winner is the first player to fill every bed. A game can last over ½ an hour, so some youngsters may get rather bored. Reducing the 'full-bed' size is one way around the difficulty.

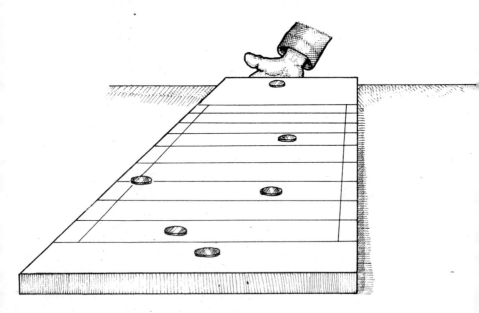

PROGRESSIVE

Like the standard game progressive is played on the specially made board. It is more suitable for experienced players, so cannot really be used as an alternative for beginners.

The difference from the Standard game is a minor one, but in play it changes the nature of play. 'Scoring' coins can be taken back and re-struck, thus a skillful player may score many of the 27 bed-places before the opponent gets a go.

31

Requiring a marking system for the board, the beds score 1-9 points. '1' is nearest the strike end of the board. The aim is to score exactly 31 points, although any other target score can be chosen. Once say a player is at 25, they must score exactly 5 to finish. A score of 7 would 'bust' and they return to the last number.

Quite fun, we found with beginners.

JACKS AND FIVESTONES

Although this is commonly regarded as a Primary School playground game, we were nicely surprised (for a change) when it created a real craze and waves of nostalgia amongst a group of 14 year olds. Unusual in this collection, it is not purely competitive, since the 'practicing' solo, takes as much time as the game. The objective is to complete a series of increasingly difficult throws with either the small coloured cubes called fivestones, or the jacks, which are small metal or plastic 6-legged objects, usually supplied in sets of five or six.

We include here the basic game and a few variants. Even if you find any fives aficionados at least having the equipment at hand won't cost you the earth!

The Basic Game

The basic throw involves tossing the stones from the palm of the hand and catching them on the back of the hand. The process is then reversed and the stones on the back of the hand are tossed and caught in the palm. **Ones** and **Twos** are games linked to the basic throw. In **Ones**, the player makes the basic throw. If all are dropped the turn ends. If one or more are caught, the dropped stones are left on the ground while the player moves all but one of the stones caught to the other hand. The single stone is thrown up and the player picks up or attempts to pick up one stone from the

ground then catching the airborne item. This is all completed with the one hand. The procedure is repeated until all the stones have been retrieved.

If successful, the player goes on to **Twos.** The second player would, on their turn go through the same process.

Twos is played by scattering the stones on the ground not too far apart. One piece is selected and this is tossed, while two pieces are picked up from the ground in the same hand. Success leads to repeating the process with the remaining two stones. **Threes** and **fours** are the same as **twos** but with a larger 'pick-up'.

Another variation is a sequence known as **PECKS, BUSHELS, AND CLAWS.**

In **Pecks,** the basic throw is attempted. If successful the player moves on to **bushels.** A catch of one or more, then involves the turnover. Holding the caught stones in the throwing hand, one stone is pushed between forefinger and thumb and this is thrown in the air while that hand is used to pick up one stone at a time from the ground until all have been retrieved and the player attempts **bushels.** In this, the basic throw again begins the sequence, success immediately moves the thrower onto an attempt at claws. **Bushels** involves throwing up in the air all the stones caught and picking up one stone from the ground in the interim. This is repeated until all the grounded stones are in hand.

Claws starts with the basic throw and if successful moves on to the ones, twos sequence. Dropping any (not all, which would end the player's turn) leads to placing all the caught stones on the back of the hand and picking up the remaining stones between each of the fingers and/finger and thumb, one to each gap. Once in position, the stones on the back of the hand are thrown and caught in the palm. Then the between-finger stones are manoeuvered from their position to the palm, completing the sequence.

JACKS

These are usually used in conjunction with a ball (small rubber type), though not necessarily so. The ball is bounced or thrown up and caught in the second hand while the sequence with the jacks is taking place in the other hand.

Over the Jump is a popular jacks game, not using the ball. The non throwing hand is placed palm downwards and 4 jacks are situated to one side of the hand. One jack is thrown in the air either from the back or palm of the hand (you decide the rule at the outset) and while the thrown piece is in the air, one jack at a time is transferred from one side of the hand (jump) to the other. Once all 4 are over the jump, the player throws the 1 jack and must make a pickup of 4. That ends the sequence.

Like with many of the games listed, if you as an adult show willing to get involved and play at a shared level, jacks can work in the most unlikely of adolescent situations. **AND** we'd point out that it's **not** just a girl's game!

6 activity games

ACTIVITY GAMES

Introduction

The fact that this section is slimmer than its counterparts bears no real reflection on how we view activity games. We do not see them having lower priority than two player games or relationship exercises. That leads us to a large BUT. Activity games in the recent past, and especially in America have suddenly become big business. Big business, that is, in the nicest sense of the phrase. Co-operative games and New Games have spawned a batch of publications and like some latter day Pied Pipers, Andrew Fleugelman, Stewart Brand, Terry Orlick and friends have been staging one day festivals of games attracting hundreds of participants. All these have been aimed at demonstrating the advantages of physical trust and fun over aggressiveness and competitive sport. The approach has won over a large number of converts and New Games' initiatives, events and 'one-offs' are currently taking place around Britain, with workers in   social work, community education and youth work heading the experiment.

We tried out a few of the games from this new source and in this section we offer these and some more traditional team games as examples of what to do with a larger group of youngsters in a gym hall or in the great outside! There is no attempt on our part either to duplicate the content of the 'New Games Book' or the 'Co-operative Sports and Games Book' or to enter the Sports arena, whereby we would find ourselves describing football, tennis and rugby. Instead, we recommend you to beg, borrow or the other thing, a copy of the New Games Book and along with marvelling at its outstanding level of production, enjoy the games described.

Finally in this section, we mention four games which are commercially marketed products. Uni-hoc, Frisbee, Swing-ball and Sling-ball are all in use in the centres we visited. They work and **as resources** they should be considered. Once tried on a couple of occasions the response can be assessed and where a piece of equipment is obviously successful then that can act as the focus for fund-raising activity on the part of the youth group. Along our route as games book compilers we found ourselves saving pennies for a second-hand pool table and a set of Uni-hoc!

FREEZE TAG

With a large group, about ¼ are designated 'IT' and they can then attempt to touch - 'freeze' the rest of the group. When touched a person must stop in the position where they have been tagged. Up until this point the game sounds rather normal and tedious, but there is a catch. All those people who haven't been tagged yet can 'unfreeze' those who have been tagged, so the inevitable result is a hall full of statues who spring to life with alarming vigour! Normally those who are 'IT' yell 'FREEZE' when touching a captive and the players who have not been tagged call 'UNFREEZE' when freeing the captives.

TUNNEL TIG

Exactly the same as FREEZE TAG, but with about 5 people 'IT' to begin with. When a person is frozen they stand with legs apart. Players who have not been 'tigged' can unfreeze them by crawling through the legs. An absolutely exhausting game, but an enjoyable one. We found it useful for 'part' of an evening session - perhaps for twenty minutes or so.

CHAIN-GANG

This version of tag turned up in the New Games Book as the Blob. We enjoyed it in the school playground and it seemed to go down well in the youth club hall.

One person is 'IT', and they try to tag another person. Once this happens they join hands and continue on the rampage. The chain becomes longer as the number of 'free' players is reduced. The chain gang can itself split up, as long as at least two people are joined together. This normally speeds up the catching process, but perhaps it reduces the fun, since a long, twisting chain gang is much more of a co-operative venture. The game finishes, or at least that round when no more free men or women exist.

VAMPIRE

The New Games people obviously went to Transylvania for this game. All the participants close their eyes and mill amongst all the other warm-blooded bodies of their erstwhile neighbours. The referee quietly tells one 'miller' that he or she is the vampire. They still keep eyes closed but as soon as the vampire bumps into another person they snatch them (no bites, please!) and let out a suitably authentic blood curdling scream. Victims become vampires and they prowl for new victims. If that was it, there would soon be a shortage of new blood, **but** when a vampire snatches another vampire they both revert to human form.

CATERPILLAR

This is another New Game. Everyone should be lying on their stomachs, side by side. The people should be sardine-like, very closely packed together. The person at one end then rolls all the way across the top of the bodies, the next person from that end following along close behind. Once the rhythm gets going the Caterpillar will make quite some speed across a hall floor or field.

An obvious extension of the idea is to have caterpillar races. For each caterpillar you need at least ten people to make it worthwhile.

EGG TOSS

This is typical of the 'Play hard, Play fair, nobody hurt' New Games philosophy. Competition is allowed and encouraged as long as its fun, but more important is the over-riding ethic that losing is fun.

Usually this is played with small water filled balloons, rather than eggs.

Played out of doors, all the players are lined up in pairs facing one another in two long lines. Each pair have their own balloon and on the instruction they throw the water-balloon across the four to five foot gap. After each round, the partners' move another foot apart. When balloons burst or are dropped that pair drop out. The last two left win and are usually invited to do as they will with their wet missile!

DODGE BALL

As with many evolving games there can be numerous versions of a game, under various guises. Dodge ball is a good example. Here are two adaptations of the game, which we have played with mixed age groups (12-18) and with a bit of supervision to prevent outright bloodshed it provides an ideal opportunity to let off steam.

Version 1

All the players assemble in the playing area. We tried it with over 40 in a slightly larger than standard badminton hall. One person has the ball and throws it at any other player, aiming at the legs, below the kneecaps. Players may "dodge" or fist the ball away. Any player may then pick up the ball and project it at the other participants, again aiming at the lower leg area. Any players hit **must** leave the playing area. The game continues (with upwards of 30, for twenty minutes or so) until there is a winner i.e. only one person left on court.

Version 2

Players are divided into two equal groups. One group form a large circle, the others become the 'dodgers', inside the circle. Play for 6 to 8 minutes with about 15 a side. The aim is for the circle players to pass the ball around and then throw it at those inside. A hit on **any part** of the body counts and that player must retire from the circle.

No 'circle' player may enter the circle, except to retrieve the ball, in which case they may not throw the ball again until they re-enter their formation.

After the time period is up, the number of 'hit' players are counted and this forms the basis for comparison, as the teams switch around.

BATTLE BALL

Despite the openly aggressive title of the game, there is virtually no physical contact between players in this game.

Two teams of 5 play one another for a fixed time, say five minutes or until all the skittles are knocked over. The playing area is divided up as below:-

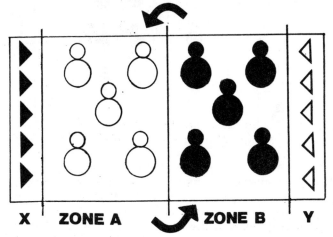

X ┊ ZONE A   ZONE B ┊ Y

No player from zone A may enter B or vice versa. Areas marked in the diagram 'X' and 'Y' are also out of bounds except for retrieval purposes. The aim is for each side to pass the ball between their players and then to aim at the skittles (which are at least three feet apart at each end of the hall).

The ball may be intercepted and it can be lobbed or rolled.

For variety, the game can be played using 2 or more balls. As a comment, we found the game very successful with 14+ and good with mixed sex groups, since, although the ball tends to be thrown with some force by aggressively male characters, the gentle, accurate lob may prove more successful in decimating the opposition skittles.

CORNER GOAL BALL

With a pitch divided as below, mark out 4 corner 'goal' areas before starting to play. As with Battle ball, each team must stay in their own half, but instead of trying to knock down skittles, the aim is to pass the ball to either of the corner goals in the opponent's half.

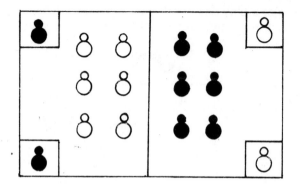

Each time the ball reaches the corner goal that counts as a goal and during an agreed time period both teams try to score as often as possible.

A rule which we tried and seems to work with teenage groups is to allow the goalkeepers to move around outside the goal area as long as they keep one foot in their area. However, a goal can only be scored by placing the ball down in the corner goal. As with battle-ball, players can pass between themselves and try to intercept shots at goal. One interesting aspect of the game, is that **after** a goal the goalKeeper must try to throw the ball back to his own team which is not always easy!

UNIHOC (imported by C G Davies and Son, Coventry)

Is it a commercial game or do we remember playing Indoor Hockey with socks wrapped around walking sticks? Anyway, this is the name of the new commercial version and for once it is a game which lives up to the claims made in the publicity handouts. The sticks are manufactured in Sweden and are made from strong, flexible polyethylene plastic which is light enough for even young players. An added advantage is that neither the coloured sticks nor the air-ball/puck which is used for the game mark the floor. Even the house-proud manager of our new local Community Centre, wore a wide smile of contentment at the end of our hour-long sessions.

The game itself is fast and tiring and the number of players per side can be varied to suit the size of the hall or outdoor area. In using Unihoc for more than a dozen sessions; we were delighted with the high level of involvement and anticipation which was present with every game. Mixed sex groups and an age range of 12-17 can easily be accommodated in the same arena as the skill and ball control inherent in hockey overcomes the basic instinct for physical aggression. In all then, a valuable asset and not too expensive. It would seem to us to be a wise investment either for individual clubs and centres or for an area worker to take around to clubs on a 'game-tasting' basis. The same firm (C G Davies) also market 'UNI-TENNIS', which is a good value for money version of indoor tennis using plastic rackets and sponge balls. It's a successfully interchangeable game, useful as a fun interlude or as a competitive sport.

FRISBEE

(manufacturer: The Frisbee Co Ltd)

Frisbee is a new game in itself and probably most families now own at least one. Here are three outdoor games which you might enjoy trying. We found that they were useful in working up a thirst!

FRISBEE GOLF

Two, three or four players bring along their favourite frisbees to a nice large open space or park. There, the first hole is agreed upon. An object, maybe two hundred yards away is the hole and in turn each player tries to reach the hole (hitting the object) in the fewest possible strokes (throws). After the first hole a new hole is chosen and each player in turn again throws for the new target. A score for the round is kept.

THROW AND RUN

While the golf game is relatively gentle, the game we developed was the opposite. The course is much the same as for 'golf'. 200 yards with a tee and a target is all you need, though we found that an ideal target might be a football goal or a sizeable tree. The thrower stands at the tee and the other player or players position themselves between the thrower and the target at a distance they would expect the frisbee to travel through the air. The thrower now launches the frisbee and the other participants try to catch the flying disc. If any of them is successful they can throw the frisbee anywhere (within the bounds of the field) they like. The thrower now scores the number of throws it takes them to reach the target i.e. eventually propel the frisbee through the goal or at the tree. A few good catches and the thrower might be up to a good score. The pace of the game tends to be fast as the thrower will usually run after the frisbee to make the second or third throw before the interceptors have positioned themselves. One other rule: the thrower must launch the frisbee from where it has landed from the previous throw and 'catchers' may not move the frisbee except after a catch or in an attempt to make a catch. They may 'stop' a rolling frisbee.

THREE AND IN

Taking the principle of most 3 or 4 player football games, the frisbee can be used as the ball while one player acts as

oalkeeper. Goalposts are ideal, but two sturdy trees can be used
ith equal success. The players each have one throw in turn and
e first player to beat the goalie three times gets a turn in goal.
handicapping system based on age and ability can easily be
troduced by setting different shortest distances from which each
layer can shoot. .

SWING BALL (manufacturer: Dunlop)

Swing ball is a competitive 2 player racket game, which can be
used indoors or out. It is easily available from sports shops and
consists of a base (which is filled with sand or water for stability)
and a pole which fits into the base. The top of the pole is fitted with
a spiral device which enables a tennis ball on a string to be
attached. When the string is positioned in the centre of the spiral,
the ball can then be hit (2 rackets are supplied) around the pole
several times in either direction without the string fouling.

Swing Ball is played with the competitors facing each other with
the pole between them. The string is maneouvred to the centre of
the spiral and one person is nominated to commence play by
hitting the ball in a clockwise direction around the pole.
The second player hits anti-clockwise, trying to reverse the
direction of play and so force the string down the spiral, until it
fouls, thus defeating his opponent.

Swing Ball is an energetic game, which can be played quite
skillfully by most adolescents.

OUTDOOR BOULES

Vaguely similar to British green bowls, this outdoor version is of
French derivation. Sets of 6 balls and 2 jacks are obtained from
good sports shops. Metal sets are expensive - plastic is cheaper
and quite adequate for most purposes.

Usually restricted to 2 or 3 players, the jack is positioned 15-20
feet away from the base. Players take it in turn to throw (not roll)
their 2 or 3 bowls, i.e. the person whose boule is nearest to the jack
scores one "shot" plus an extra one for each of his boules that is
closer to the jack than the nearest of his opponents'. The second
jack can be positioned at base, and play resumes for the next

round.

A useful piece of equipment to have handy when spending time outdoors, e.g. at a campsite or barbecue.

INDOOR BOWLS

Such equipment is expensive to buy, but can usually be found in community centres. Simply an indoor version of green bowls, a pile carpet is necessary to play on. Bowls is a fascinating game and its worth trying it at least once in a group's life, to see if it catches on.

Remember, though, that its a poor substitute for green bowling which can be tried during the summer months.

7 commercial games

COMMERCIAL GAMES

Introduction

Ignoring the fact that this book has a kids' eye slant to it, and ignoring the fact that the selection of the games, the organisation of chapters and the writing up is quirky and personalised, you may still find the inclusion of this chapter unusual and unexpected. If any area of gaming is ignored or afforded low status, this is it. "The store-room is the place for the monopoly and scrabble" - that is the over-riding opinion. If it can even be seen as such a positive action. Rather, boxed games of the commercial variety are scorned and neglected. Few see the light of day and rarely do we witness youth and/or group workers involving themselves in playing such games. Ultimately, this produces its own set of consequences. Rules are not learnt, and when in a state of abject boredom some youngster or other goes to borrow a game, pieces are missing, or the accompanying odds and sods are chucked around, symbolically displaying frustration at not being able to properly play the game, yet, unaided and unable to find any way to use and enjoy the resource.

A major difference in the way we have written up this chapter, which separates it from the rest of the book, is in that **we do not offer sets of rules and tips on play.** In no sense do we intend to infringe copyrite, nor do we think that rules without the board or playing pieces is particularly logical or useful. Instead, we have experimented with the games in different settings and in this section we have tried to capture the essence of the game, i.e. "a sophisticated ludo" or " the beginnings of military strategy in warfare". Added to this short description we have attempted to formulate our subjective responses to using the games as a means of entertaining young people in association with adults.

We know that no two youth work situations are exactly similar, so our broad comments may be too general to have applicability to your club or group. On the other hand, the positive or negative comments which we make may give indications as to whether the games might be useful for your work place.

Our sessions with youngsters in I.T. groups; YOP workshops and youth clubs were within an open, voluntary framework. No-one was compelled to play, but it developed naturally in an unhurried spontaneous sort of way. We were with the games and in a way we were part of the games. The bits of plastic and card are not the end of the tale, many of the youngsters wanted the attention of the adults and the relationship angle of play can hardly be over-stressed. Even one-player contrivances like maze games become group activities. "Can you do it, Howie?" "What's the aim of this one, Alan?" become the immediate verbal indicators of the shared nature of the playing. Many are also shared experiences in the sense that they are designed for a number of players. Some require physical dexterity and are essentially doing games, like the water games, the maze puzzles, close the box, rebound bagetelle and baffle box. Others are geared to learning a technique, which relies more on brain and timing.

Scrabble provides a test of literacy, but with fun, and it is a good game , which is of paramount importance. The boxed games made by Waddington's, Ideal and others, we found suffered from one basic fault, which in a way is ours, not theirs. The games are long - too long for many players to be both fully involved and allow for a change of participants. We like playing Monopoly, Risk, and Formula 1, but neither the formal or informal youth group work situations seem to be terribly suited to the playing of the extended and extensive race game.

Two player games, such as Othello, 2001, Cul-de-sac and Mastermind were, somewhat surprisingly avidly devoured as players queued for anything up to half an hour to be next "on". We also briefly imported a T.V. game, but these are rather delicate pieces of equipment and unless you have a rich benefactor they cannot really be recommended for youth work, despite their captivating appeal.

In essence, we saw this chapter as completing the total picture of games with young people. Our only omission is the organised, traditional team game, the football, hockey, cricket arena. Many of these must not be discounted since they are central to the British sporting heritage and as such provide a fine vehicle for involvement and a means of dissipating aggression.

Once taught to a couple of kids, most of the games we have written about can be passed on, using monitor-style procedures. The selection criteria we used, in the main, was, can it be learned easily? Where the answer is yes, games have been included. We hope you enjoy them with the youngsters in your own groups.

You should consider introducing groups to your own favourite commercial game(s) be it 'Backgammon' or 'Go'. Neither of these two games are specifically mentioned in the book, but we have seen Backgammon being successfully introduced to kids by an adult 'addicted' on the game. If an adult is enthusiastic about a particular game, this enthusiasm can often be passed on to kids, resulting in them becoming 'hooked' on a particular game. But beware! - Crazes can start this way, and before you know it you may have a whole group heavily into Backgammon, or whatever!

CLOSE THE BOX

(various manufacturers)

This is a traditional game, re-packaged for commercial sale. As a teaching aid it is a good introduction to numbers and at the same time seems to be popular with most young people. A simple idea, the box has the numbers 1 to 9 inscribed along the inside and above each number is a flap which can be turned over to cover the number. Two dice are thrown and the total indicates the value of flaps which can be closed up. Say, a total of 9 is thrown, then any of the following combinations of flaps may be closed.

9 = 8+1; 7+2; 6+3; 2+1; 5+4; 5+3+1 and 4+3+2.

That player continues to throw the 2 dice until either they cannot use part of the total score, or all the flaps have been turned over. In the version we used, 6 small ball-bearings are provided for each player. The numbers left uncovered at the end of the game give the number of balls to be given to the opponent. At the end of a turn, the other player repeats the process.

It sounds mundane, and it is, but it has a strange sort of appeal, and can be played by any age and takes just as long as the contestants want it to. There are quite cheap versions of the game on the market and if you go for a strong one it should last for years.

SUBBUTEO FOOTBALL (manufacturer: Subbuteo football)

11 year old Alberto persuaded us to include this one as a good game for the more organised youth club. Played on a five foot long green cloth, the game involves "finger-tip control" of the 11-a-side football teams, which compete for a fixed period of time, 2 halves, say perhaps ten minutes each way. Set out on a table top and firmly held down the game can be played by a number of participants and features all the normal rules of football, goals, penalties, fouls, throw-ins etc.

Club-championships have been organised in some centres and a league-table structure could be established where the game is popular. Probably the better mannered members of the voluntary organisation run clubs, boys' movement etc are the best setting for this activity or its near relation, the table top war games. This again requires special equipment, soldiers, dice and rulers - but you'll have to read about the finer points elsewhere!

Returning to Subbuteo football, our advice is for centres considering purchasing a set, to consider buying the "Club Edition" which has the basic needs without the extra paraphernalia gone in for by the enthusiast.

REBOUND (manufacturer: Ideal)

An activity game, this is closely allied to the traditional game of Shuffleboard. Produced in quite sturdy plastic with metal, low-friction playing pieces, the game is at least strong enough to be 'let out' unsupervised. In the following diagram the shape of the board and the path of movement for the players' 4 pieces is shown.

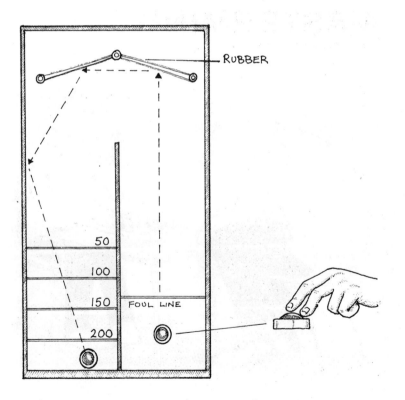

RUBBER

50
100
150
FOUL LINE
200

Pieces are pushed up the table and the two-players shove one piece alternately up the board. The rubbers at the top end of the board act as a cushion and the pieces re-bound down the left-hand passage into the scoring area. Only pieces inside each scoring line area count, so part of the game is to nudge your own pieces on to score and push the opponent out.

It seems to work and be appreciated as an activity wherever we tried it. Like other games used, it produced its own waiting list and queue of users. The sides of the board are used as a score board and it can be played either by 2 players, or in teams. We got bored by it rather quickly, but the same was not apparent amongst the younger users. It's funny but if the same board had been made of a nice block of teak, I think that we adults would like the game more.

People **are** strange!

MASTERMIND
(manufacturer: Invicta)

Suffice it to say that most people have played this 2 player game at some time. The basic principal involves hiding 4 coloured pegs under a shield and then the other player tries to find out the hidden sequence by testing coloured pegs and being told non-verbally by the placing of black and white pegs, whether any are in the correct sequence. After about 8 tries, normally a player finds the original combination.

Nowadays, most of the youngsters have seen and played Mastermind a bit too often and although the original idea is a unique one, it has palled somewhat with over-use. Suggestions which we have tried are (1) to add 3 or 4 extra colours, or (2) combining 2 boards together to play a double game with a code combination of 8. Both make for a more difficult game, but not doubly difficult; it usually takes about 1/3 more tries to find the winning line. (3) consecutive games can be played with two boards.

Age-wise, we would reckon 9 or 10 upwards and the time for a game of one guess each is about fifteen minutes.

There are also word and number versions of the basic game but we feel that the rather poor quality pieces might easily get lost   with youngsters using them.

THE BAFFLE BOX
(manufacturer: M & B Games)

A test of memory, the game is played fast with each player, from 2-6 in number, putting a marble into one of the 36 holes in the top of the box. One marble in a hole disappears; a second in the same hole is returned to the unlucky contestant. The winner is the first person to successfully get rid of all their marbles. There are other rules regarding the numbering of the 6 rows and instructions for choice of rows, what action to take when rows are full etc. Anyone over the age of about 5 should be able to play.

We found it a good "one-off". A second game began to pall and left to   their own devices the game was forgotten amid a melee of rattling marbles. That said, if a youth project has a budget for games **and** a turnover of users/members, or whatever, then the game is original enough to be worth having. A minor annoyance we encountered with out set was connected with the size of the balls - they varied from being correct to too large, which in the course of a game means that two balls in a hole may both stick, instead of the second one falling through. Annoying and confusing and, one feels, rather unnecessary.

BAGATELLE
(various manufacturers)

This was a Victorian pastime and the wooden tables, normally made with a semi-circular top are available either through the games and toy shops or in second-hand shops, where £2 may get you an antique as well as an enjoyable game. The idea, which has been translated into simpler, plastic copies, is to knock (or in some versions, shoot with a spring-trigger) ball bearings into a variety of cup-holes and segmented areas made from tacks nailed into the board. Most boards look something like:

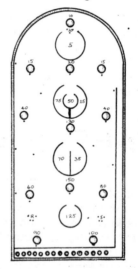

The balls are knocked around the board and when all have been used the score is totalled and other contestants have their turns. About 3 turns each with up to 4 players makes for a good game. It is refreshing to see youngsters getting pleasure from an old-fashioned pastime. We were lucky in having 2 other early twentieth century bagatelle type games. They were more like prototypes for pin-ball and therefore, if anything, were even more popular.

Kids of all ages enjoyed the game and although it might not be a piece of equipment you would want to use every week, the acquisition of bagatelle can be a boon. New models tend to be £10 plus and made of a far inferior wood to old models, so the junk shop suggestion can be beneficial.

WATER GAMES
(manufacturer: Tomy)

We are not going to suggest drowning all the kids in your care although you may sometimes (often?) feel so inclined! Instead, the water games we are referring to are 8" square boxes filled with water. There are at least five different varieties, basketball, starball, ring-toss, triangle-toss and tic-tac-toe. Of these we found that all intrigued but while some were intriguing in an aquarian sense, i.e. transfixing the stare, others were skillful, especially the ring and triangle models.

Even babies could play with these machines, but obviously since pre- and post-conception "preventive" work hasn't quite appeared yet, we were using the "wonderful waterfalls" as they are called with kids in their teens. Pushing the button on the front of the box sends a stream of air into the water which moves balls, rings or whatever around in the water. The aim then is to manoeuvre these missiles into or onto targets. It's more difficult than it sounds and quite addictive if not used in isolation from alternative pastimes.

Youngsters can compete using the games singly and then comparing the scores. Most of the games have an 'out of play' area, so scoring can be counted **against** each player. Not a bad investment, since they seem to be fairly well made, and as long as they are not used as the ball in touch rugby, they should survive a school year, or so.

SCRABBLE (manufacturer: Spears)

This old game has become one of the most beloved of family recreations. We have also found that most projects and centres we visit have sets and use them. The game, as most people know, involves placing words, one letter to each tile onto a board with marked squares. These squares on the board indicate when the score of words are doubled or trebled and likewise with individual letter tiles, which are each numbered. Words must join on to letters of words already on the board. The winner is the person who has the highest score when the tiles run out at the end of the game.

Most children from about 7 upwards, can, in a limited way play Scrabble, but in adult company (up to 4 can play) they'll get a mite hammered. So, with kids holding a limited vocabularly we use a 4 or 5 **maximum** letters in a word rule. This acts as a leveller, although it obviously decreases the enjoyment for the adults. A good painless way to increase the vocabularly. We found that the game worked better in a slightly quieter environment of group work rather than in a youth club setting. The game does last a bit longer than we would normally recommend for kids' groups, probably in the order of 1½ hours, but only an hour where kids play without adults. These older people even 'ruin' Scrabble, you see!

If a club is **into** games at any level, Scrabble is a must.

MONOPOLY AND CLUEDO

(manufacturers: Waddington)

The 'dodos' of the Games Scene. Both are still purchased consistently and provide hours of fun and aggravation. In the case of Monopoly it is literally hours and hours, and we always use either the shortened version mentioned in the Waddington rules, where 2 properties are dealt immediately to each player and a time limit is established, or a version where 4 properties are given to each player which **they don't have to pay for.** This moves the game on by about 3/4 hour. Monopoly because it is universally known can still provide a valuable group experience and the interaction which takes place may lead to the same sort of de-briefing and group discussion which we have talked about in the relationship games section.

Cluedo is a short game, played in twenty minutes sequences and involves deducting who is the criminal, what implement they used for the crime and where it took place. The movement around the board is made by dice throw and then one hears improbable statements such as "I suspect Colonel Mustard in the study with a rope". This is inevitably followed by a humourist who will say: "I suspect the Reverend Green with Miss Scarlet with a candlestick". Shades of Ken Russell! It's a good game and although the rules take a few minutes to explain it's not difficult to learn.

185

OTHELLO
(manufacturer: Peter Pan Playthings)

From the makers of 2001! Actually it's the other way round. Othello came first and is one of the games highly esteemed by Games Players (those persons who fancy themselves as a sort of playing elite). So simple, the game can be taught in a three minute burst, but the chips, which are double sided, black on the face, white on the reverse can be placed in such a way as to ensure victory or doom. Only two can play. Enclosing a line of the opponent's colour, turns that line over. White becomes black or vice versa. At the end of 64 squares the board is filled, black and white discs are counted up and the winner is the person with the most pieces of their colour face upwards. Possibly the diagram at the bottom of the page helps to explain the layout of the game.

Intriguingly, although the game takes about five minutes to generate momentum, it has proved itself well as a youth game. The Centre Manager of one local Community Centre has played very little else since the game was introduced!

The duration of a game is approximately twenty minutes. The age spread of players is from about six upwards.

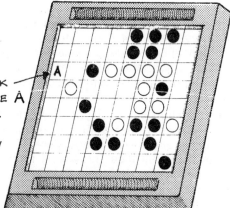

PLACING A BLACK
PIECE ON SQUARE A
WOULD TURN OVER
THE WHITE PIECE
DIAGONALLY BELOW
AS IT BECOMES
'ENCLOSED' IN THE
BLACK LINE.

2001 (manufacturer: Peter Pan Playthings)

Every year, one game maker or another produces yet another variation on tic-tac-toe. Waddington's tried it with "Cube-Fusion" - a frankly forgettable epic. 2001, for 2 players is more successful using a magnetised board with 5 x 5 squares. The board itself is interchangeable so that the magnetic squares can be moved around to confuse the player who attempts to memorise the magnets. The aim is to make a row of 4, and each of the playing pieces is a clear plastic dome with a red/yellow, two-sided magnet enclosed within. When placed on the squares these may stay the same or change colour, so playing a piece may give the opponent a piece of their colour.

This seems to be one that will last in terms of interest and enjoyment - based on our tests in 3 successive sessions. Unfortunately, our opinion is that the magnetic strips which make up the board will quickly disintegrate in normal youthful use. Possibly some sort of covering might strengthen them. It rather depends upon the effect this might have on the magnets - it would also need to be carefully executed to ensure that one piece is not recognisable from another.

MAZES (various makes)

The traditional ball bearing puzzle was a popular toy in the period between the first and second world wars. An 18-hole golf course game and 'Road Race' games were particularly popular. In the sixties and seventies the ideas were revived using clear plastic casings. Many of these involved balancing the small ball-bearing on a raised ledge and manipulating it around the raised path to the end. Others used the old fashioned pathway principle where the aim is avoid falling down the holes cut into the pathway. Pocketeers have recently introduced one such model where a path is followed and the ball must be moved into a small boat and across a river, up and over bridges and through other hazards. It's not the best made puzzle we have seen, but it's a good idea and we would recommend the **Pocketeers** as a range of small, cheap toys worth considering. The only drawback we can see is that being small, they also fit neatly into small pockets, **leaving** buildings!

The time taken to complete a puzzle or do and re-do it is unlimited, depending on the patience and determination of the user. The Los Imposibles puzzle by Congost of Spain is one we have seen 19 year old bikers spend an evening fiddling with   and a five year old girl complete in five minutes. They are very personal things and can be thought of as annoying and frustrating by some youngsters and adults.

At the top end of the range are the Swedish wood mazes and 'Round the Bend' made in plastic by Invicta. Both are expensive and use the principle of two handles, which, when turned change the angle of the playing board and so the ball moves. The aim is to avoid the hazard holes. If unsuccessful, the ball falls down a hole and that point score is the player's total. They are hard enough to provide a real challenge.

We liked the way that the mazes could be used. They can be left on tables and passed around between youngsters, and they don't require the setting up or rule learning of other games. Also they can be played between any number, age or ability range of youngsters (and adults). The, "Want to see if you can beat me at this?" invitation from a staff member will often work where other ways of starting a conversation have failed.

CUL-DE-SAC
(manufacturer: Lazy Days)

This is a two player game on a plastic board which is divided by slits in horizontal and vertical directions.

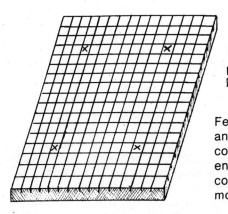

Fences are given to each player and two men are started from corresponding points at opposite ends of the board. Each move consists of placing a fence and moving one 'man' two spaces.

In this way men are diverted by opponent's fences and they retaliate in kind. The winner is the first person to capture one of the opponent's base squares. It's quite fascinating to play and appeals to the 14 plus age group especially, although it is easy enough for 8 plus to learn and play. If pieces get lost it 's rather annoying, but the board is reasonably well made. Waddingtons used to produce a fence game of their own called "Kimbo" but probably because the cardboard playing surface used to get damaged by placement of the fences it was discontinued. A game of Cul-de-sac lasts about quarter of an hour and by the end of that time you and your opponent will have seen some of the most obscure corners of the board!

YAHTZEE (manufacturer: M & B Games)

Ingenious, simple and hybrid. Sounding more like a description in a rose catalogue, rather than a game, Yahtzee has its roots (excuse the pun) in Poker dice and simple scoring games. Although it is a so-called 'Commercial Game' the only equipment needed is a set of 5 standard dice and a pad of score sheets, one of which is given to each player . Unlike some other games in this section, it can be played by any number from 2 to 6 with equal success.

We found that it worked in a variety of group settings, both formal and informal. A game lasts about half an hour and once learned it is an easy game to just "leave about" and then, with the minimum of supervision the monitor principle takes over, one youngster explaining the rules to the others.

Like in Bridge, (for games freaks), the scoring is achieved in 2 sections above and below the line. Each player throws the 5 dice and tries to "score" in a section of the scoring table which hasn't been filled in. Any number of dice can be thrown 3 times and then either a section must be scored or a section is "blocked in", indicating that the player cannot or does not want to make a score elsewhere on the pad. The sections to be scored are Aces; Twos; Threes; etc and then as in Poker dice, straight runs; full house; 3 & 4 of kind and Yahtzee which is 5 of a particular number, say 5 x 3's. A score over 63 in the 1-6 section, above the line gives a Bonus score of 35. Every section must, by the end of the game, be 'scored' or 'blocked off'. The winner, predictably, is the person with the highest score. There are other rules, but that's the basics. A good game which is quite skilful, but once watched it is usually easy enough for kids to master.

TWISTER (Manufacturer M & B Games)

With action all the way, Twister is most definitely a 'doing game'. Played in stockinged feet, the contestants entangle themselves and one another on a plastic sheet playing surface marked up with coloured circles.

A master of ceremonies calls out a colour and part of the anatomy, left or right hand or foot to that colour. The decision is made mechanically by a spin of an arrow. The end result of the proceedings is a knotted, laughing heap of bodies. The number of players in sessions which we were organising varied between 2 and 6. When we weren't involved, the apparatus tended to be used as the means to get into the Guinness Book of Records, with upwards of ten folk piled, pyramid-style towards the ceiling.

Great as a "one-off", we also found some indication that the game could be played on a regular basis for 3 or 4 sessions. In itself a fun idea, the commercial game, like its close-relation, 'Knots', can be used to break down some of the physical inhibitions of group members.

8 simulations

SIMULATIONS

"In the beginning..." as all good books say, we mentioned that we are not one hundred and one percent 'sold' on the use of simulations and roleplays at every opportunity. Some of our professional colleagues like Tom Scott, who   helped towards this collection **are** convinced and use the techniques at many staff development sessions and interestingly in I.T. groupwork and in training and fun sessions with youngsters in the 14-20 age group.

Anyway, our sour grapes out of the way, we would like to commend 'Starpower' and the 'Tower Game' to you as fairly well-honed training simulations ideal for conferences, team meetings and the like. Both require briefing and de-briefing and a certain quantity of equipment as listed in the game descriptions. Starpower is analogous to the class struggle or just keeping one's head above the water-line. Strong emotions can be aroused and don't think that it is your handling of the group if participants opt out and temporarily disappear. Acquisition and doing down your neighbour and some measure of knowledge concerning how rules are made and broken all come into a normal session. In contrast, the Tower Game is a group exercise and the groups are locked into competition with one another to build the most financially advantageous tower. The game is well worth playing with older kids' groups as well as in a staff context. As a 'doing' exercise, it is fun, and a good, money producing tower will have involved the builders in an amount of lateral thinking.

'Highland Survival' is a survival exercise of a type piloted in America. As well as presenting an identifiable exercise/game to the participants, whether they are adolescents or leaders, Highland Survival provides some of the ingredients of real, live information necessary to would-be hikers who 'do it wrong'. We found the simulation successful with both youth club kids in the 14+ age bracket and I.T. groups. Since the exercise is scored, some sort of carrot, i.e. a Mars Bar or something can be offered as a prize.

STAR POWER GAME

And after Star Trek and Star Wars, here it is, Star Power!

You will need the following equipment:-
(1)   Supplies of coloured tiddlywinks (or counters of some sort)
(2)   Copies of the rules of bargaining
(3)   Blackboard and chalk
(4)   Labels showing triangles, circles and squares

See Rules of Bargaining for values of the chips (tiddlywinks etc)

Method:

The group is divided into three, giving out labels of triangles, circles and squares. Prepare 3 bags of counters beforehand giving each participant five counters, loading the total value in favour of squares, less to circles, and positively handicap triangles. Allow ten minutes for trading. (see rules of Bargaining).

Send participants back into their groups, put individual scores on the blackboard under groupings. Without giving any reason, give each group three counters telling them that each scores twenty points, and the counters may be distributed among the group in three ways, two ways, or all to one person. When these new scores are put on the board (members who have received some or all of the sixty points have their scores changed) re-arrange the groups so that those with the highest scores go into squares, any low ones go into triangles, and the rest go into circles, trying to keep the groups reasonably even in size. (When members change groups they must, of course, change their labels as well). Take back the counters worth twenty points and repeat the process as long as you like.

Participants tend to go through three stages:
(a)   This is a joke but I will go along with it.
(b)   I'm a bit involved but it's only a game.
(c)   I really mind about what is happening.

After about 3 or 4 rounds, when the squares have got thoroughly established, you can allow them to make one or more new rules (e.g. they may change the value of the currency, or they make make new trading rules).

You must decide how long you allow the game to continue, depending on how much feeling you want to generate, and, particularly with young people, you must have time for reflection.

Points to Consider

What are the:

(1) Comparisons with the real social structure.

(2) Assumptions of going up and down, (i.e. improving your score means getting **more** points, the squares **win** etc).

(3) Feelings of members of the groups on moving up and down, or not being able to move, or not wanting to move, opting out etc.

(4) Reasons behind who keeps to the rules and who doesn't. What rules do the squares change and why?

RULES OF BARGAINING

1. You have TEN MINUTES to improve your scores.
2. You improve scores by trading advantageously with others.
3. Persons must be holding hands to effect a trade.
4. Only one for one trades are legal. Two for one or any other combinations are illegal.
5. Once you touch the hand of another participant, a chip of unequal value or colour **must** be traded. If a couple cannot consummate a trade they may have to hold hands for the entire ten minutes trading session.
6. NO TALKING MAY TAKE PLACE UNLESS HANDS ARE TOUCHING.
7. Persons with folded arms do NOT have to trade with other persons.
8. ALL CHIPS MUST BE HIDDEN.

BLUE	50
PINK	25
GREEN	15
YELLOW	10
WHITE	5

5 chips of same colour - extra 25
4 chips of same colour - extra 15
3 chips of same colour - extra 10
2 chips of same colour - 0

THE TOWER GAME

Budding Basil Spence enthusiasts are especially welcome in this game.
A pre-arranged incentive (prize) should be awarded to the winning group.

The **aim** of the game is for each group to work as a team and produce the highest tower in the fastest time using the fewest bricks. Extra **PROFIT** will be gained by teams who **estimate** accurately the height, bricks and time they will need to build their Tower.

There are two phases in the game -

Phase 1:   Groups are chosen and in a period of up to an hour the groups work separately on the tasks indicated in the Planning Phase.

Phase 2:   is the construction phase and the time allowed for the Simulation is X no of groups multiplied by 20 minutes.

1.   **PLANNING**

The groups may join bricks together, but must dissemble before entering the construction Phase. Each group is given a collection of LEGO including base plate and approximately 50 bricks of the 8 blob variety. The group tasks are to:

(a)   draw a design of the tower to be built indicating the method of joining the bricks.

(b)   estimate the profit (see separate estimate chart and incentive graphs), time taken, height of tower and bricks used.

(c)   make a plan/description of who is expected to take what part in the construction phase.

2.   **CONSTRUCTION**

Up to 20 minutes will be allowed for each group to carry out the following tasks:-

1)   Introduce and describe the plan.
2)   Brief group members.
3)   Build the tower (stop-watch timed) using the base plate and 200 bricks.

4) Measure the completed work against the estimates and the incentive graphs to arrive at a **profit record.**

After all teams have engaged in the construction activity, the team with the highest profit record is declared the winner and group discussion, as desired can take place.

The Profit Record is the total profit gained in incentives for speed, height, careful use of materials and bonuses for accurate estimates.

INCENTIVE GRAPHS

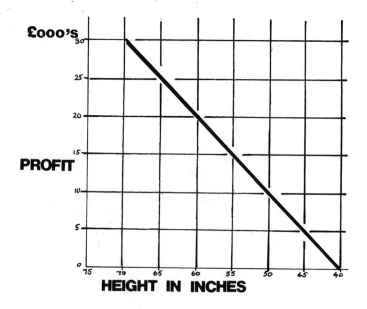

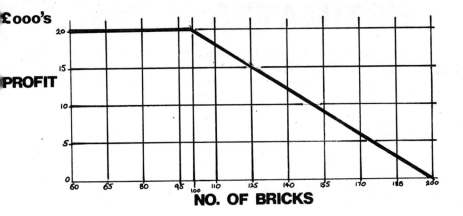

£ooo's

PROFIT

NO. OF BRICKS

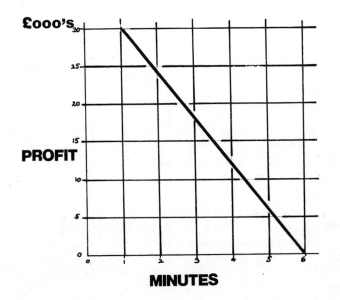

£ooo's

PROFIT

MINUTES

ESTIMATES

Estimates regarding height, time and bricks used carry the following bonus profits:

Height	40-50"	51-60"	61-75"	
Accurate within 7"	£3,000	£4,000	£5,000	B O
Accurate within 3"	£4,000	£5,000	£6,000	N U S

Time	Under 1	1-3 mins.	4-6 mins.	
Accurate within 10 secs	£6,000	£4,000	£3,000	B O
Accurate within 30 secs	£4,000	£3,000	£2,000	N U S

Bricks	151-200	101-150	Under 100	
Accurate within 10 bricks	£2,000	£3,000	£5,000	B O
Accurate within 5 bricks	£3,000	£5,000	£6,000	N U S

HIGHLAND SURVIVAL

Instruction: Divide the participants into groups of 4 and supply each individual with a full set of these instructions and the map. Each person must have a pen and each group should have a spare 'group copy' of the instructions and tables. The Co-ordinator of the exercise should introduce the situation and briefly "set the scene". The whole exercise will last about 1½ hours.

The four of you have got yourselves in a mess. It is late October and you have set off on a hiking and camping holiday in the Cairngorms in the Highlands region of Scotland. After catching a train to Aviemore, you hitch hiked up the ski-road as far as Loch Morlich and hiked into the mountains. On the first day you reached refuge at **Ford of Avon** and on the second the ruin on the banks of the river Avon having spent the day on Ben Avon. It is now the end of the **third** day and you have been stuck in your tent for twenty-four hours since it started to snow. The weather, up until the evening of the second day had been mild, but a decrease in visibility was accompanied by a rapid drop in temperature. Snow started to fall at about 8 p.m. on that second evening and with only short breaks has continued to do so right up until now. You are worried since the position you camped in is far from ideal. The shortest route to the nearest help is by foot path to Cock Bridge and this means a trek through the snow of 6-7 miles. Visibility is down to about twenty-five yards, a north easterly wind, force 6 is blowing. The temperature is remaining in the range 27°F - 36°F. The snow is two feet deep over all, but drifting makes the conditions treacherous, especially since it is newly laid and walking is difficult in soft snow.

You are faced with a series of choices. Regretably, your group did not inform the Police of your route before setting out and with the poor visibility no-one will find the tent in the forseeable future. The weather shows no sign of improving and one of your group is beginning to suffer from hypothermia. It seems that your only chance of survival is to send one, or more of your party to get help. How many of you should go? What equipment should you take? What should you leave with the tent? These choices will probably mean the difference between survival and disaster for the 4 of you.

FIRST TASK

How many of you should go for help? Without conferring, tick one of the 3 choices in the INDIVIDUAL Column 1

Table 1

	Indiv. (1)	Group (2)	Expert (3)
1 to go			
2 to go			
3 to go			

Penalty Score =

TASK TWO

There are twenty items of equipment/supplies in the tent. Choose TEN which should remain in the tent and TEN which should be taken.

RING THE TEN WHICH ARE TO BE TAKEN ON THE JOURNEY TO OBTAIN HELP (See Table 2)

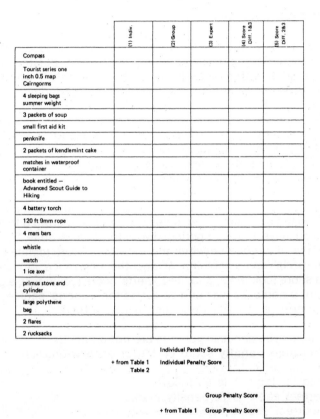

	(1) Indiv.	(2) Group	(3) Expert	(4) Score Diff. 1&3	(5) Score Diff. 2&3
Compass					
Tourist series one inch 0.5 map Cairngorms					
4 sleeping bags summer weight					
3 packets of soup					
small first aid kit					
penknife					
2 packets of kendlemint cake					
matches in waterproof container					
book entitled — Advanced Scout Guide to Hiking					
4 battery torch					
120 ft 9mm rope					
4 mars bars					
whistle					
watch					
1 ice axe					
primus stove and cylinder					
large polythene bag					
2 flares					
2 rucksacks					

Individual Penalty Score

+ from Table 1   Individual Penalty Score
Table 2

Group Penalty Score

+ from Table 1   Group Penalty Score

TASK THREE

Individually and without looking at what the rest of your group write, PUT A NUMBER INDICATING PRIORITY against the ten items you are taking with you on the journey, i.e. if you ringed compass and torch and think that these are the 2 most important items write a **1** against compass and a 2 against torch. Continue **1 to 10** until all the ringed items are in order of priority.

TASK FOUR (on separate Group sheet)
All 4 members should now get together and look at Table 1. Discuss **as a group** how many of you should go for help. Once you have reached a decision, put your tick against your choice in column 2 Group.

TASK FIVE (on separate group sheet)

Repeat tasks 2 and 3 working as a group to choose which **ten** items should be taken on the journey. Then, put·the ten into priority order. Complete these tasks and task 4 above on a separate sheet to avoid confusion with the underlining.

The co-ordinator of this exercise will now read out to you what the experts would do in this situation. Mark the experts' score into the columns provided in tables 1 and 2.
Compare your choices and scores with theirs.
Is there a very big difference?

If your choices are similar to theirs, you would probably have survived the situation. Fill in columns 4 and 5 on **table 3** to find out how you have done. Scoring the difference is done by writing down the difference between the Individual score (column 1) and the Experts' score (column 3) and the difference between the Team score (column 2) and the Experts' score (column 3), e.g. if you thought a compass was choice **3** and the Experts' choice was **1**, the difference to write in column 4 would be **2**.

If the items you chose in your ten are **not** on the Experts' list, score a **difference penalty** score of **10** for each wrong item.

Scoring for table 1 is as follows:
(1) correct choice..NIL penalty marks.
(2) incorrect choice..TWENTY penalty marks.

CO-ORDINATOR'S NOTE

The value of this type of survival exercise is in knowing what choices might be in front of you if you ever do find yourselves caught out on a mountain-side. It also gives a practical indication of a group making a decision, compared with the individual. Most times when this exercise is used, the group will score a far lower (i.e. better!) score than individuals. The competitive element in the exercise between individuals and teams of 4 ensures that the exercise will appeal to youngsters and will not be too divorced either from other games-play or the reality of hiking.

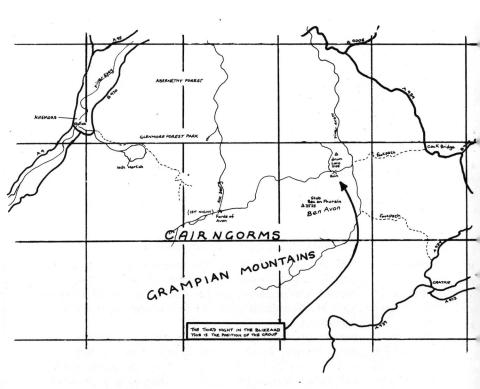

EXPLANATORY SHEET (to be given out after the exercise)

TASK 1

Two of the group were recommended to go on the trek for help. This was because:

a)   it leaves one behind to look after the person suffering from hypothermia

AND

b) the pair are likely to become less frightened and work together better than either might as individuals in a similar survival situation.

TASK 2

Items in priority order:-

1. Compass
2. Map
3. Rucksacks
4. Polythene Bag
5. 3 Mars Bars
6. Watch
7. Rope
8. Torch
9. Ice Axe
10. Whistle

Reasons for above list:

Item 1:   Essential for accurate route finding.

Item 2:   Necessary for reading the landscape; evaluating distance and to use in conjunction with compass.

Item 3:   Necessary for carrying other items. Can also be used for sitting on/foot and leg protection from cold, if benighted.

Item 4:   For easily obtainable shelter from snow storm/ deteriorating weather and for use if benighted.

Item 5:   A good psycholigical thing to have, occupies mind, reassures person by the fact of having it. Increases energy level quickly.

Item 6:   Useful for judging distance covered etc. Prevents distortion of time.

Item 7:   Useful for keeping in contact with each other in bad visibility - river crossing - hand line if confronted with a steep drop.

Item 8:   If benighted, it is useful to have as a psychological aid. Handy for giving SOS signal whilst walking, in case someone is nearby.

Item 9:   For testing the depth of snow, using as a cutting instrument, and if both persons are joined by a rope it can be a useful aid for the front man in windy weather.

Item 10: If lost, will certainly last longer than torch for giving SOS signal.

The position of the tent is known, therefore as long as the two who are remaining stay put, they will be rescued. The Kendlemint cake and soup will be enough to keep them alive for a couple of days and the sleeping bags are absolutely necessary for their warmth and survival. The matches, stove, soup and penknife for chopped Kendlemint cake dissolved in water (as a drink) all fit together as a package. The book and the flares are a psychological aid and the flares may also be useful if rescuers are heard.

Our thanks to Louis Isbrand and Frank Grant for their assistance with the preparation of this simulation.

BIBLIOGRAPHY

1. Theory of Games

(i)   B De Koven
Interplay Games Catalogue. (Intensive Learning Centre, 5th and Luzerne Streets, Philadelphia)

(ii)   G I Gibbs
Handbook of Games and Simulation Exercises (E & F N Spon 1974)
An extended bibliography, which must be treated with caution. With the speed of things changing in this arena, the collection is already rather out of date.

(iii)   Don Pavey and Michael Challinor
The Art based Game as a mode of Education (1976) and the Art Arena Games Pack (1978) c/o School of Liberal Studies, Kingston Polytechnic, Penrhyn Road, Kingston Surrey KT1 2EE

(iv)   S.A.G.S.E.T.
The Society for Academic Games and Simulations in Education and Training. Can be contacted at 5 Errington Moreton-in-Marsh, Gloucestershire

(v)   D Watts
Simulations and Games with 'Less Able' Pupils can be contacted through S.A.G.S.E.T.

2. History of Games

(i)   Arnold Arnold
The World Book of Children's Games (1976) (Pan)
Using historical principles, this games book concentrates on the younger age group and is best for reference in the sections on "ball, bowling, beanbag and balloon games" and "Strategic board games".

(ii)   Michael Bentine and John Ennis - Book of Square Games, (Wolfe Publishing 1966)
The source of much mythical endeavour.

(iii)   E Berne
Games People Play (Penguin 1970)
A pleasing collection of psychological relationship games with some historical material.

213

(iv)   Edward de Bono
         The Five Day Course in Thinking (Penguin 1972)
         The originator of lateral thinking in a do-it-yourself
         guide.
(v)   Edward de Bono
         The use of lateral thinking (1971) Pelican
(vi)   Edward de Bono
         Po: Beyond Yes and No (1973) Pelican.
(vii)   J Strutt
         Sports and Pastimes of the People of England
         (first published 1801. Republished 1969 Firecrest
         Publishing). A marvellous introduction to the history
         of British games.

3. Relationship Games

(i)   Blatner H B (ed)
         Acting in Practical Aspects of Psychodrama
         Informative and valuable as an introduction to this
         field of work with games.
(ii)   D Brandes and H Phillips
         The Gamesters Handbook (Hutchinson 1977)
         Each game is well described and aims, materials and
         variations are adequately explained. We liked the
         format, though we haven't yet seen the paperback
         version.
(iii)   Larry Butler and Lex Allison
         Games, Games (Playspace 1978)
         A useful collection of cards, together with a short
         pamphlet/book on areas of use. The format is good;
         the material could do with more commentary regard-
         ing how the sequences work in different settings.
(iv)   J Canfield and H C Wells (Prentice Hall 1976)
         100 Ways to enhance self concept in the Clasroom
         aimed at teachers and parents, the book applies the
         Gestalt theory to teaching and offers a range of
         practical exercises through which kids can develop
         an understanding of themselves and a better self-
         image.
(v)   Cockpit Arts Workshop
         Warm-Ups and Ice Breakers (Alec Davison, Cockpit
         Arts workshop, Gateforth Street, London NW8 8EH)
         A nicely produced large leaflet with many valuable
         games and role plays.

(vi)   M Harrison and the Non-Violence Children Program
         For the fun of It: Selected Co-operative games for
         Children and Adults (1975)
         A good collection and overlook at games in a co-
         operative setting.

(vii)   Robin Holtom
         Imagination Games (Springfield Hospital, London
         SW17, 1976)
         A couple of duplicated pages of art therapy games.

(viii)   Jeff Merrifield and Pat Eyre
         Startlers (Essex Community Education Service)
         Quite a nice set of duplicated sheets in the
         group/arts/drama section. They fall quite easily into
         the Icebreaker's section of games-play.

(ix)   Panmure House
         A Handbook of Group Games and Techniques
         (Panmure House 1978)
         "So You think you can play Games?"
         This was the 'bible' for relationship games, but the
         nasty I.T. Resource Centre (us) gobbled their material
         and included it in sections 4 and 5.

(x)   The Panmure House Compendium of Games
         "So you think you can play games" was extracted
         from this comprehensive collection of games and
         groupwork techniques. Access to this source was
         invaluable.

4. Indoor games, puzzles and travelling games

(i)   R C Bell - Board and Table Games (O.U.P. Vol 1 1960
         and Vol 11 1969)
         A comprehensive, if rather stodgy collection of board
         games, it gives little idea of how valuable one game is
         compared with another. Perhaps they hadn't tried
         them! (offstage cries of "heresy")

(ii)   Gyles Brandreth
         The Hamlyn Family Games Book (Hamlyn paperback
         1978) One of the "what you can do on a journey or
         wet day" variety. Intelligently put together, as
         befits the author, though a little thin on the content.
         There's a good puzzle section at the back which we
         photocopied and used with groups. Yet another
         copy-rite infringement!

(iii)   Gyles Brandreth
Indoor Games (Teach Yourself Books 1977)
Well organised as a collection, the material covered echoes some of the sections in this book. You may find one or two new Parlour Games.

(iv)   Maxey Brooke
Coin games and puzzles (Constable 1973)
Really rather a boring, self-opinionated presentation, **but** it does include some original games and puzzles.

(v)   Jonathan Cape 1977
100 Amazing Magic Tricks
Translated from a turn of the Century French tome, this collection is visually uplifted by original lithographs. Many are impossible to build; lots are hazardous, **but** the whole publication fascinates most teenage readers.

(vi)   The Diagram Group
The Way to Play - The Illustrated Encyclopaedia of the Games of the World (Bantam 1977)
An amazing book in every sense of the word. We found it invaluable and there's still plenty of fascinating material for you to browse through. The diagrams are faultless, the coverage is as near comprehensive as is humanly possible, and the rules are, in the main, clearly explained.

(vii)   Joseph Edmunson (illustrated) Pan Books
The Best Party Games
Provides comprehensive range of party games for all ages and situations like Beach Parties, barbecues etc.

(viii)   Martin Gardner
Mathematical Puzzles and Diversions (Penguin 1961 & companion volumes)
Only to be dipped into for youth work use. Most of the contents are far too esoteric.

(ix)   Eve Harlow
101 Instant Games (1977 MacDonald)
Nicely illustrated and a varied collection. Some of the games descriptions are rather brief, but Larry's cartoons do wonders for the presentation. Worth having a look at.

(x)   Vladimir Kozian
        Mazes (Pan 1972)
        If you are looking for something different to leave
        around, this might be it. Used with tracing paper or
        photocopied, the book itself could last some while.
        The contents are mostly quite difficult, so the result of
        frustration might be a shredded book!

(xi)   Marshall Cavandish 1978
        The Bumper Fun Book
        With 365 things-to-do, this is the most interesting,
        well presented collection that we have come across.
        Good for 10+ age group. Recommended.

(xii)   Jerome Meyer,
        Puzzle Quiz and Stunt Fun (Dover Publications USA)
        An old-fashioned collection of puzzles and party
        items. Dated, but still of some interest.

(xiii) Hubert Phillips
        Pan Book of Card Games (Pan 1960)
        Old fashioned, yet quite satisfactory as a collection.
        As a complementary source to the Way to Play, it can
        be a useful item to prop up the bookshelves.

(xiv)   Ronald Ridout
        Puzzles Galore. (Dragon Books 1976)
        For younger kids, it is a fill-in-the-missing
        picture/sentence variety of book. Not bad.

(xv)   Richard Sharp & David Pritchard
        Christmas Crackers, (Sunday Times, Xmas 1979)
        Lots of quick puzzles, games, card games and
        patience.

(xvi)   Arthur Taylor
        Pub Games (Mayflower Books 1976)
        A valuable collection of the normal and the odd, many
        of which we have usefully used in the youth and
        social work setting. Amusingly written and readable
        as a whole.

5. Group and Activity Games

(i)   A Fluegelman
        The New Games Book (Sidgwick and Jackson 1976)
        The ultimate in production technique, and overall a
        human and readable collection of alternative games
        you can use with groups of youngsters and adults
        ranging in size from 2 to a collossal 1,300 in the case
        of the Lap Sit record! Recommended.

(ii)   T Orlick
         The Co-operative Sports and Games Book
         Writers and Readers Publishing Co-op (1979 Britain)
         Mostly for younger children under twelve, but some of
         the material can be used in a mixed age setting.

(iii)   Roger Hope and colleagues
         Kids! (NAYC)
         An excellent source book for those working with
         younger kids. The booklet includes dozens of useful
         games in addition to a wide coverage of other
         worthwhile group activities.

6. Simulations

(i)   Sarane S Bookock and E Schild
         Simulation Games in Learning (Sage California 1968)
         (see especially Dale Farran's section "Competition
         and Learning for underachievers).
         One of the early writings on games which is a part of
         the academic backdrop to the New Games era.

(ii)   Alec Davison and Peter Gordon
         Games and Simulations in Action (Woburn Press
         1978). Simulation in the educational setting would be
         a better title. Most useful for Youth Social Work is the
         section on the making of Simulations.